T0266389

All Set for Black,
Thanks.

ALSO BY MIRIAM WEINSTEIN

Yiddish: A Nation of Words

Prophets and Dreamers: A Selection of Great Yiddish Literature

The Surprising Power of Family Meals: How Eating Together Makes Us Smarter, Stronger, Healthier and Happier

All Set for Black, Thanks.

A New Look at Mourning

Miriam Weinstein

SHE WRITES PRESS

Published 2016
Printed in the United States of America
ISBN: 978-1-63152-109-6
Library of Congress Control Number: 2016932854

Book design by Stacey Aaronson

For information, address:
She Writes Press
1563 Solano Ave #546
Berkeley, CA 94707

She Writes Press is a division of SparkPoint Studio, LLC.

Permissions:
Excerpt from *Mahzor for Rosh Hashanah and Yom Kippur*, 1978, p. 241 with the permission of The Rabbinical Assembly.
Excerpt from Breaths, Lyrics adapted from the poem by Birago Diop, music by Ysaye M. Barnwell © 1980. Recorded by Sweet Honey in the Rock.
Who By Fire, Words and Music by Leonard Cohen
Copyright (c) 1974 Sony/ATV Music Publishing LLC
Copyright Renewed
All Rights Administered by Sony/ATV Music Pubishing LLC, 424 Church Street, Suite 1200, Nashnille, TN 37219
International Copyright Secured All Rights Reserved
Reprinted by Permission of Hal Leonard Corporation

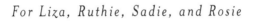

For Liza, Ruthie, Sadie, and Rosie

" . . . What we have loved,
Others will love, and we
Will teach them how."

—WORDSWORTH

"I think that Joy has a great idea of keeping an outfit all together in a garment bag in the closet. The last funeral that we went to . . . there were young girls in spaghetti strap tanks and shorts, which I was surprised at because it was in a Mormon temple. I think that I and a friend of mine were the only ones in any black at all. I had a hard time figuring out what to wear, and I had already started thinking that when I get to my goal weight I want to put together an outfit for occasions. Oh wait – we went to one after that and "everyone" was in black (except me)."

youlookfab.com

TABLE *of* CONTENTS

PROLOGUE:

IT'S US NOW: SNATCHED *from* LIFE

"SHOULDN'T IT BE HEATING UP BY NOW?" I STOOD IN my friend Mitch's kitchen one brisk autumn evening denying, against all evidence, that my coffee pot was dying. "It takes a long time," I stalled. But at a certain point I had to admit that the signs were not good.

It may seem extravagant to own a thirty–cup urn, but it is only expensive in terms of storage space, not cash. Over the years, its steady burble has provided a comforting background through dinners, committee meetings, holidays, happy events and, of course, the occasional *shiva*, the period of mourning that Jews observe after a death. That's what was happening at Mitch's that night. The house was filled to bursting with people worn through with grief. And, while the wine seemed to be serving many of them just fine, there were an awful lot who would have died for a cup of hot coffee.

We were all more or less in shock, needing to be together, incapable of letting this go. Mitch, the center of so much of the life of our small city, had died a couple of days earlier, two and a half weeks after checking into the hospital with stomach pains and yellow eyes. He had been feeling poorly all summer, but not even poorly enough to go see the doctor. The diagnosis was pancreatic cancer.

Evidently, the complications from this kind of disease can be the thing that gets you. "They're killing me in here," Mitch had said to his wife, who has been my friend for decades. Of course the medical team was trying its darndest to do just the opposite, but even one of the world's leading hospitals—with all its named pavilions, labs, operating theaters, a helicopter pad on the roof—could not prevent his death.

The funeral the day of the coffee pot failure had filled City Hall, to the point where those of us on the ornate balcony of the post–Civil War auditorium were beginning to feel anxious about the weight, listening to the creaking of the floorboards, eyeing the wrought-iron supports. That night, everyone felt the need to come to the house that had been a gathering place for so many great times, with the large windows that Mitch had cut so they could have a view over Good Harbor Beach.

My friend Kim, who had met the family at my kids' weddings, caught up with me in the kitchen. She just wanted to offer a hug to the new widow. I understood her impulse, but here was the problem: If everyone just wanted to give a hug, that made for a thousand hugs, a thousand people in a living room that could comfortably hold maybe half a dozen. (Okay, if you added the eating area, the kitchen, and the foyer, you could get up to twenty or thirty.) People were squashed, nibbling on desserts, happy to see folks they hadn't seen in years, feeling weirded out by feeling happy. Every once in a while I would take the cover off the coffee urn, stick my finger in the water in the hope that we were making progress. We weren't.

The rabbi showed up with the box of books for the prayer service, often a strange focus of a strange evening. If there is any kind of crowd, there are nowhere near enough books, so there is a lot of huddling and sharing. And, while some people run through the mostly Hebrew prayers at a good pace, others try to look concerned or at least not confused, while some just give the whole thing a pass and resume their whispered conversations, their eating and drinking, their greeting of long-lost friends.

Mitch was a central figure in the Jewish community, although his actual beliefs were somewhat less than orthodox. He was also a densely-connected therapist, former carpenter, actor, and the heartthrob of his year at Gloucester High School. If he had been present, he might have been busy praying, or he might just as likely have been busy schmoozing in the rear, vastly enjoying either mode, rocking back and forth on his heels. After the prayers, he would have placed his hand on your shoulder, commiserating and half-laughing, but dead serious, saying, "Yeah yeah, this really sucks."

People were reluctant to leave the house and, as they spilled out onto the street, they didn't want to get into their cars. We huddled together, as if we could protect ourselves from a future that all of a sudden looked bleak. The night got dark and the autumn breeze got cold, coming in off the beach. We talked about how we would keep tabs on the family, go see our doctors, kiss our loved ones; how we would manage our own futures without Mitch.

It is tough enough to be a mourner, someone whose world has just been ripped open. And sometimes our friends, despite the best of intentions, don't really help. Nobody in their right mind wants to go around thinking about dying all the time, and we live in a world that certainly doesn't encourage it. For many of us, the old ways, whatever they were, were jettisoned long ago. We want to do something, but we have no idea what is "right" or "appropriate."

So we bring casseroles. ("Sushi!" one family member said that night. "Why can't they bring sushi?") So we blather platitudes. So we look for "closure." So we worry about saying the right thing and, being embarrassed or shy, say nothing. We explode in grief over the deaths of people we hardly know, or have never even met. Years on, we are still at risk of being sideswiped by grief, trying to knit some kinds of coverings over the holes that open when a loved one dies. And each successive death reminds us how thin, how fragile, those coverings really are.

None of us gets out of here alive and, unless we die young, we will see a lot of people go before it is our turn. And we will remake our lives without our beloved ones, our supports, our buddies, again and again.

I learned this the way that fortunate people do—with grandparents, moving on to parents, then watching you-know-who come and snatch away first one friend and then another. Even if it is "expected," when it happens, it hits us over the head like a mallet blow. Sure, some things help, but not always the things we expect.

So the trick at this stage of life is not how to get into college or find a mate or figure out a career; it's how to deal with this onslaught, and not in some pious or (you should excuse the expression) deadpan way.

And yes, humor helps. At the raucous Irish wake for my friend Jeanne's father, one of his pals looked over at him, lying silent in his coffin and noted, "He never did mix well at parties." At my own father's funeral, one of his distant cousins showed up loudly and enthusiastically chewing gum. We hadn't seen the guy in years and could barely remember his name, which didn't matter, because for us he became, ever after, The Gum Chewer.

Here is just one of the treasure trove of available jokes: Two friends loved to play baseball. After one dies, the other one is delighted to have a visit from his deceased friend. "So tell me," the live one asks, "Is there baseball in heaven?"

"There's good news and bad news," his friend replies. "Yes, there is baseball. But you're going to be pitching tomorrow night."

I wrote this book as a series of essays following the shock of Mitch's death. It became a collection of thoughts about how we handle death in our culture, as well as a way to let you know about my own dear ones who are gone. And, of course to give advice: what *do* you wear to a funeral? What *should* you say when you are certain that anything you say will be wrong? How do you deal with the question of the ashes? Who gets the broken but beloved (name your own memento)? How do we keep our dead with us even as they drift farther away? How do they become us, just as we become them? I mostly stuck with what and who I know, except for some side trips into weird mourning practices I couldn't resist. The hope that fuels this kind of enterprise is that the personal will become universal.

The writer's mantra is: tell me about your Italian grandmother, and I will understand my Polish grandmother. (Warning here: Just wait until you meet my Russian-Jewish one!)

That night at Mitch's, I finally dumped the lukewarm water from the coffee urn into the sink, and took the pot back home. I thought: maybe I can get it fixed. I thought: I've had it for a million years, but it still seems like it went way too soon. The next day, tired of thinking, I heaved the old pot into the trash.

I then embarked on a more-or-less year-long search for meaning. (Good luck to me!) But I began the year by splurging on a new coffee urn. The only thing that I could be certain of was that, given my demographic, the odds were good that I would be needing it again.

What *to* Wear *to a* Funeral:
All Set *for* Black, Thanks

I BOUGHT AN EILEEN FISHER DRESS ON SALE SEVERAL
years ago—a soft wool jersey with a neck that kept me
warm but did not scream *turtleneck*. It was relatively long and
relatively full. I am on the short side, so I try to avoid things
that come off as being too much dress, but this was nicely
pared down, and it suited me well. I will let you guess the
color.

I bought it thinking that it would be cozy in winter, and
would be appropriate for lots of different situations—workish
events, some kinds of going out, some versions of what I think
of as state occasions. I was not thinking funeral specifically
when I bought the dress, but when, that first year with my
new purchase, my uncle Dave died in the middle of a frigid
January, one of my first thoughts about the funeral, to be held
in a northern suburb of New York City, was: *thank God I have
the perfect thing to wear.* (In my defense I will note that Dave's
side of the family constitutes the most stylish branch.)

That soft black dress, plus tights, boots, down coat, serious hat and gloves, got me through the kind of day that Dave knew and did not love. He had grown up in southern Canada and northern New York state. His first job out of veterinary school was in a village in the Depression-stalled Adirondacks where, he said, "You haven't lived until you've stuck your hand up the inside of a cow who's giving birth when it's minus twenty"—that would be Fahrenheit—"and you're being paid by a little old lady with a jar of nickels." From that point on, his professional life went south, which in his case did not mean it deteriorated; quite the opposite.

So in his honor, and because what would be the point of suffering anyway, I was glad that I was dressed warmly and presentably for standing around in the gray, frozen cemetery while my uncle was being buried. Foremost among the mourners was my cousin, Dave's daughter, who had flown in from California with her husband. They were not taking well to the cold. Although they were lifelong New Yorkers, and had only recently moved to L.A., they seemed just as shocked by their sudden re-immersion into winter as if they were real Californians. They kept fingering their old, but still quality, lined leather gloves. Afterwards, in the restaurant and the adjoining lobby of their copiously-decorated suburban hotel, we all got as close to the fireplace as we could. We had made it through the day, and we needed that little hit of warmth, solace and light.

Looking good may not be as directly beneficial as a warm fire, but it can make you feel good, and feeling good can make you look good (which, in turn, makes you feel better.) These may seem like obvious truths, but they can be forgotten in times of extremis. We run around thinking about all the things that have to be done to deal with the death, to prepare for the funeral and mourning period, and then to cope with all our friends and loved ones who are also in various throes of grief. Or we are unable to do anything at all, so others circle around us while we barely move. This is not the time to be rushing to the local department store, having a meltdown in public because some half-noticed detail reminds of you of something you just cannot bear to contemplate when you are trying to put together an outfit, all of which is happening while you are in no condition to face yourself in the mirror. Honestly now, wouldn't it be better if you had that dress already hanging in your closet at home? I have a friend who is as caring and decent and loyal as they come. She shepherded her own dear friend through her last illness, and then missed the actual moment of death because she was in the mall, buying something to wear to her funeral.

Just as we eat or drink to soothe ourselves, we might as well do what we can in the image department to help us through this vale of tears, which is a good description of acute mourning, and which is how traditional Christians charac-terize life on earth. I prefer the point of view expressed in the Yiddish proverb, "Man comes from dust and he ends in dust. In the meantime, a shot of vodka never hurt."

Being prepared is a good beginning, although you don't want to be the kind of person who stands around in front of her closet thinking, let's see now, do I know anybody who is likely to be dying soon? If so, what season would that be, and how am I fixed for black? This problem is more likely to be an acute one for Jews, who have to bury their dead within a day or so, leaving precious little time to borrow something from a sister or friend, or to run out to the store as described above. Even if you are not in the first line of mourning, it is difficult enough to buy clothing for a very specific event. No one wants to do it on deadline.

Luckily, the what-to-wear conundrum has become a little bit easier in the years since our collective love affair with black. This has now outlasted several economic cycles and presidential administrations, as well as our obsession with vampires, which makes it difficult to believe that it "means" very much. Life is too complicated? We want to look thin? We are in a decades-long depression? If you do have any ideas, don't hesitate to let me know.

Especially if we live in urban areas, we are likely to have a closet full of black, gray, navy, and dark brown – the hues that, in an earlier time might have caused a friend to say, hey, you look like you're on your way to a funeral. So the problem gets narrowed down to cut, style, and suitability.

If you are the type who goes in for classic tailored subdued clothing at all times, or if you work in finance, you can probably stop reading right here. Flight attendants might also be okay, if they leave off the parts of their uniforms that have wings. This is for the rest of us who are flummoxed by the whole idea of owning drab clothing, are too creative for our own good, are into statement dressing, or are several pounds heavier than we were the last time this subject came up.

If you are in deepest grief and shock, or you are one of the mourners with a reserved front row seat, you are probably not thinking too much about your wardrobe, unless you are irretrievably superficial and image conscious (that would be nobody I know, and would certainly not include me). In that case, it might cross your mind that you, and your grief, will be on full display. As you shuffle into the good seats when everyone else is craning their necks, as you sit there drawn and sniffling, as you walk up the aisle after the event, as you grip the arms of your loved ones at the gravesite, all eyes will be on you. And since this is probably the only public occasion at which no one will be taking photos, they will not be distracted by gadgets. They will be looking. And they will be remembering. Decades later, my friend still recalls the woman who came up to her at her father's funeral and told her that her father would be ashamed of her—her skirt was too short!

May I also suggest that your outfit be comfortable and appropriate to the weather, to the grassy or dusty cemetery ground, and to a lot of sitting and standing around? Because no matter how efficiently things go (and this is one occasion where efficiency is not a high priority), you will be wearing that outfit over the course of what will probably be a very, very long day. If the weather is cold, you will be overcome by shivering. If the weather is hot, you may well swoon.

Even if you are not in the immediate circle of mourners, you are dressing for an intensely public occasion. It is one of the times when our inner state is expected to be expressed by our outer appearance. No matter what our standard approach is to clothing, this is one time when we are expected to pretty much blend in. When the bereaved look up, they should see a sea of black. Okay, maybe not literally. But they should have the sense that they are being supported, that their own grief is front and center, and that people are there to help them, not to call attention to themselves. (And yes, the truly vain among us know that even pulling off that *I'm just fitting into the crowd* look can be a form of self-congratulation.)

But what is it with the black, anyway? It is a pretty standard symbol of mourning because, well, the absence of light is so obvious. Victorians brought this concept to a state of high art, or at least obsession. In wealthy families, when the head of the household died, even the servants were outfitted in mourning. Widows faced years of stringent rules around what they could wear as well as do. Pity the widow in deep mourning, which lasted a year and a day. She had her choice of many different fabrics, as long as they were all dull black. And No Ornamentation! None! Any time she went out in public, she had to wear a weeping veil, the better to sob without making a spectacle of herself. Things improved, though, during what was called second mourning, which lasted up to nine months. Fabric trim! Mourning jewelry! The jewelry was made of the hair of the deceased, or else of jet, which is nothing but a shiny form of coal. But there was the possibility of color, if only purple, mauve, and gray, to break up all that black. And, in a nod to human decency, those women who lived in the tropics were allowed to wear white. We won't even discuss the next phase, half-mourning, here.

Americans didn't go quite that far. One exception was in the defeated South after the Civil War. Following the brutal carnage—of the more than six hundred thousand soldiers killed on both sides, two-thirds were Southerners—so many Southern women were wearing black that people feared the entire region would sink into depression. At one point, the governor of Mississippi tried to pass a law against wearing mourning clothes, but grief, or at least the stylized expression of it, won out.

We would like to think that we don't believe in such things any more, but in fact we do. If funeral clothing were not so carefully prescribed, we would not be having this discussion now. Our clothing is highly dictated by social norms even though we are always going on about individual freedom, individual expression. We might chafe against the rules, but we tend to stick close to them.

Because rituals help us move through our lives. We may find ourselves obsessing over what to wear to a funeral that doesn't much matter to us. At the ones that register high numbers on our own seismic scale, though, we cannot even think about how we look. Either way, we are in the midst of grief, either living it or acting as part of the living backdrop. The quiet garb signals *yes, I know.*

But that subdued *just being there* attitude is not really our cultural forte. Is it any surprise, then, that funerals are becoming more casual, more individualized? At a themed funeral, a golfer can expect to be sent off to the afterlife from his favorite hole. At such an event, it would only be natural that a few golf shirts would make an appearance. A cookie baker's funeral was held in a funeral home, but the room included her collection of cookie jars and her stove. Aprons, anyone? As time goes on, it will only become more likely that you will be invited to a funeral where you are asked to wear a Hawaiian shirt or a disco outfit. (I am not making up these examples.) Just beware the invitations that say costume optional. How embarrassing would it be if no one took up the offer except you? Or if everyone did, and you were still wearing your tedious tasteful suit?

Special circumstances: Going to a funeral in Florida,

something I have done twice now, requires some thought. You know that you are supposed to wear black, or at least bleak, but the problem is that it is SO HOT there, and the prevailing aesthetic, once you leave South Beach and head out to the tribal reserves where the very old people tend to live—and are therefore where you are more likely to be going for a funeral—the look is more pastel, with white, or pale, accessories.

Luckily, a mark of conspicuous consumption in hot climates is over–air conditioning, so the funeral homes hover at suit weather, leading you to think, maybe I was even supposed to wear pantyhose. And the old people I have known have opted for cremation rather than burial, so, for my two Florida experiences, there was no standing around in the hot sun.

Side note: I have noticed that really, really old people, the ones who are most intimately connected to the dead, and who presumably attend the most funerals, often dress the worst. They tend not to be into buying new clothes; the ones they bought decades ago strike them as being good enough. And comfort comes first. Sometimes I think that the process of aging should be called the time of progressively more sensible shoes.

I could not tell you what I wore to the funerals that were truly awful for me. Luckily, some of them were so long ago that there is no reason for me to remember. But even for the more recent ones, I have pretty much blocked out those details.

Because whatever you wear to a funeral that gets you in the gut has the possibility of taking on Meaning. This is not so likely if, say, under normal circumstances you wear lots of black and this is a funeral that is not a life-changer for you. But let's just say that you don't and it is. What, oh what, did poor Monica do with her blue dress in the aftermath? (What happened to her was a sort of death.) What would Jackie have done with the pink suit that she wore in Dallas, if she weren't the First Lady? Those are examples of two bodily secretions you will hopefully not have staining your own funeral attire, but still—what will you do with the outfit that you, metaphorically or not, drenched with your tears?

Your choice is to wear it aggressively, effectively bleaching the mourning out of it just as Victorians did once their official period of grieving was over. Or you can go the other route, sticking it in the back of your closet and never wearing it again, a sinkhole for unbearable feelings. Because you know very well that, every once in a while, when you are rushing to find something to put on for work in the morning, and everything you might normally wear is dirty or doesn't fit or is somehow unappealing, that death dress will be the one that you find, and there goes that day.

So I will tell you about that long black wool jersey dress. Maybe because fashion has moved on, or maybe because it was a bit of a strange purchase to begin with, I have not gotten a lot of wear out of it. I have a summer black dress that's great for travel, and I wear all the time; likewise a couple of black sweaters. But that black wool dress? It hangs in my closet. It has not gotten any less warm, cozy, soft, inviting. But although it has been several years since my uncle died, I do not think I have worn that dress again.

WHO GETS *the* SPOT NEXT *to* MOM: ETERNITY *in* JERSEY

*H*ERE IS HOW I GREW UP THINKING ABOUT DEATH: It was the proximate cause for our outings to New Jersey, and my introduction to spinach pie. I grew up in the post–World War II Bronx, and even though (because?) my parents had done a fair amount of moving around in their early lives, once they established themselves in our neighborhood, weekend trips beyond the borough required some logistic and psychic effort. One of our regular destinations was the cemetery.

The trips began when I was four, when my father's mother, a non-smoker, died of lung cancer in the apartment she shared with her husband, daughter, and son-in-law. I have only one visual memory of her, lying in bed. I think I put talcum powder on her very soft skin. My father loved to describe how, when she died, I went into the room and lifted up the sheet to make sure she was dead. He told this as a funny story, so I decided that it must have been humorous. Now I think, hey Dad, that wasn't funny; it was natural for a kid. I also think:

my aunt would have been the person caring for her at home. How did she feel about that? And my father was her doctor; something that nowadays would probably be illegal. But now that I am thinking about it, of course there is no one left for me to ask.

At the time, my parents, who were death virgins, joined in with my aunt and her husband on the purchase of a spacious ten-person corner plot. That uncle had waited until his own mother died before marrying my aunt. Once the New Jersey plot was purchased, they moved her from, as I recall, Queens or Brooklyn, to the more spacious and suburban reaches of the Jersey cemetery that was just being developed by people like themselves—Eastern European Jewish immigrants and their children. Many of the plots were communal, bought by benevolent associations defined by their shtetl of origin, or else by a trade or a political leaning. Most of these things—the shtetls, the trades, the splinter political groups—no longer exist.

Also, the death virgin idea may be overstating things slightly. My father was a doctor, an old fashioned general prac-titioner, my mother an operating room nurse, so you might say that for them, death was part of the job. But they had been spared the personal losses of normal growing up, as well as the generational loss of the Holocaust. Their own parents had left Europe as single young adults, and so my parents had only a remote concept of what a grandparent would be. We also, luckily, had no immediate family killed in the War.

The drive out to Jersey began by packing seven of us into the car (this was way before seatbelts) and beginning our stately approach—past Yankee Stadium, across the mighty

Hudson over the great George Washington Bridge, with my father reminding us how there used to be no bridge, but only a ferry, and my mother making sure that we waved to the Little Red Lighthouse, charming and long-outdated, at the edge of the Manhattan shore.

Once in Jersey, civilization fell away, and we stopped at something we called the duck farm. (Why? I remember no ducks. Maybe it was just a way to have a break on the long car ride.)

The cemetery was a vast flat expanse divided into streets, where we managed to get lost every time, despite the grid layout. It was almost as bad as Queens, which, because the streets and roads and avenues have numbers, lulls you into a false sense that there is some logic you might, with luck, discover. In the cemetery, we didn't get our bearings until we sighted the flag pole and headed for it. When we were almost there, we would stumble upon our corner.

Our headstone said Weinstein, centered, and under it Nerson, which was my uncle's family name. My grandmother and my uncle's mother each had her own footstone. The headstone was pretty plain, although the top curved. I liked some of the fancier stones better; they had images of flames or books. But we had a bench, placed catty-cornered, which made a good place for the grown ups to sit on, or for us kids to use in our play.

My father would open the trunk of his car and unwrap his hedge clippers, which were swaddled in old greasy towels. He would methodically cut the hedges that surrounded the graves, *clip clip clip*, the tiny bright green leaves falling on the grass. We paid the cemetery people good money to do this, but obviously their efforts were not sufficient.

Looking back, I am guessing that my father had mixed feelings about his mother, and that it was helpful for him to have a job to do, even if was a made-up one. She does not seem to have been a particularly warm person. There may have been reasons—orphaned at an early age, made to work as "a slavey," my father's term, for relatives when they were still in the Old Country. But she did manage to make it over here, find a nice man to marry, then travel back and forth across the U.S. several times, doggedly advancing the welfare of her husband and children.

So that is Lena's story. She was born, she lived, she died. She was buried in New Jersey, along with her *makheteneste*, the Yiddish word that means the mother-in-law of one's child.

While we stood around the grave, and my father worked on his sprucing up, I don't remember anyone talking about the dead, or even being sad. I would like to think that I was being sensitive or observant, but I was probably only interested in running around, eating, and going to the bathroom—a trait I see in my young granddaughters now. I do have a very clear memory of the ladies' room at the cemetery office, which had a strange chalky smell.

I also had a cemetery job of my own. It is a Jewish custom to leave a small stone on the grave, to show that you have been there (no better explanation seems to be available, even though this custom has acquired a sense of obligation.) Since it was the only activity possible while the grown ups stood around, my sister and I made the most of searching the ground for attractive pebbles, comparing the number, placement, and general appearance of our stones to the stones on other people's graves. When you hear about poor children in the past, or in undeveloped countries, having only rocks to play with (my other grandmother told me how, in czarist Russia, that was how they used to play Jacks) it sounds pathetic. In my memory, though, placing the stones on the grave was one of the highlights of the trip, and I'm not saying that in a bad way. It combined serious work, aesthetic judgment, treasure hunt, serendipity, fun.

Quite often, after the cemetery, we would visit old friends of my parents who lived nearby. These were the only people I knew who lived in the suburbs. Their house was a classic child's drawing of a Cape. They had a real backyard. The mother wore slacks and, for all I knew, drove a car. The kids had strange names, Candy and Buddy, which my parents never failed to discuss on the ride home—how my father's old friend, the husband, had married somebody perfectly nice, but Not Jewish, and how it was killing the friend's mother, an immigrant like theirs, to have to call her grandchildren by those ridiculous names. (You already know that my parents named me Miriam; you don't know that my middle name is Ruth, and that my sister is Naomi. My parents might have been strongly anti-religious, but that put only a scratch in the armor of their Jewish identity. Indeed, a strong anti-religiosity is the hallmark of a great many Jews.)

The cemetery visits might have eased up through my later childhood and early teenage years, or maybe I started skipping them. Then, in the fall of my junior year in high school, my mother's father dropped dead of a heart attack. Throughout my mother's childhood he was continually deserting the family, then showing up and expecting to return to his spot as the stern father in charge, then deserting them again. My mother's explanation was that he had come from a relatively well-to-do family in Russia. He could never accept the fact that he had to start from the bottom once he got here—the opposite of the immigrant success story.

Around the time my mother was getting married, her father landed in L.A., where he found a wealthy widow he wanted to marry. My mother and her siblings convinced my grandmother to divorce him, leaving out the part about the wealthy widow. The wealthy widow did not pan out, but Charlie remained in California alone. During my childhood he was a legend, a secret, a subject of tall tales, a locus of regret. But now he was dead, and the family needed someplace for him to go.

My mother and her siblings bought another plot in the Jersey cemetery, not so nicely located as the Weinstein head-quarters. The Barsky plot is in the middle of a row, near the main road. I cannot believe that they did this. This is a family with a strong visual streak, people who cared a lot about how things looked and felt. Their spot is so bland compared to the spacious, quiet Weinstein corner plot with its bench I can only assume that they had no choice, that the cemetery was filling up.

When Charlie's body arrived by plane from California (exciting in and of itself), the family opted for a graveside service, but the rabbi was late, so we all stood around in the chilly November afternoon. Nobody wanted to talk; there were so many wounds that had been so poorly bound and opened again and rebound over the years. And this made it final: things would never work out. Charlie's ex-wife (my grandmother) and two older children hadn't had any contact with him in decades. The two younger children—my mother was one of these—had kept in touch. The one time he visited us, we were careful not to mention it to the rest of the family. I remember him as being extravagant: walking to the bakery to buy jelly donuts for breakfast (my parents were much too health-oriented ever to have done that), and teaching us to write in an elegantly shaded calligraphic script.

But now my aunt and my grandmother were sniffling hard into their embroidered handkerchiefs. Finally my uncle Dave, the oldest son, a man who was capable of long periods of silence, who had carried back shards of delicate china from bomb-blasted Hiroshima, opened a book and recited Kaddish, the prayer for the dead.

The teenaged me was heartsick, not because I was upset about Charlie (the only thing his death meant for me was a canceled sleepover with a new friend), but because of what I saw playing out in front of me. This was a family that worked hard to project spunk and a can-do attitude, to contain pain in funny anecdotes. That day, no one had the heart to try out the old stories. No one said, *good thing he's gone.* No one said, *poor guy screwed up his life; look at this wonderful family he could have had.* No one said a thing.

The most recent funeral was for my aunt Shirley, who died in her sleep in her early nineties. My uncle found her in the morning. I was one of the first people he called but, because of a cellphone glitch (Why then? Why me?), the call didn't register on my phone until maybe five that evening, by which time I was already insulted that I had been left off the list.

Shirley was buried in the Barsky plot, the second family

plot, the one near the road. Already buried there: my grandfather Charlie (first in), my beloved grandmother Millie, my aunt and uncle who I was also close to—they had no children of their own. Now that Shirley is there, her husband Morrey talks about going in the spot next to her.

He adored her, as did her two sons and, more impressively, her two daughters-in-law, who stood at the graveside sobbing and comforting each other. (Impossible not to think —will my children-in-law one day be sobbing for me? I had better start being nice to them.) But mostly I thought about how, when Shirley married into the family fifty years earlier, no one gave her a break because she was—well, there's no good way to put this—so Midwestern, so unstylish, so earnest. She was League of Women Voters in a family who, when they were poor, really *did* take down the velvet living room drapes to make a dress for my mother to wear to a dance. (If my mother later became a nurse, she became a nurse with panache. Her white nurse's dress always had a flattering fit, the seams in her white stockings were always straight.)

Now when I look at the grave groupings, they seem quite arbitrary. Shirley, the decent woman from Illinois, gets to spend the rest of forever in Jersey with her in-laws. My mother is a five minute walk or car ride away (if you can spot the flag pole and head toward it) with *her* in-laws. Their fourth sibling, Dave, is buried a good hour away in Westchester, with his wife. That spot was chosen because, when Dave's wife died, that charming cemetery, more wooded and rolling than the New Jersey one, was more convenient and more appealing for their only child. Unfortunately, that only child moved to California, where *her* offspring live. She hates to travel. She flew back East for Dave's burial, and has not been back since. As far as I know, nobody has ever visited the grave.

I can see how Hindus or Buddhists might opt for the idea of a dead person moving on to a different state, or how Christians might focus on some time when, in some unspecified way, we will all be together and, better still, we will all get along. I can even understand the Zoroastrian tradition of leaving a body in a tower in the open air to be plucked clean by vultures. Jews can come up with a vague concept of The World To Come, but it's something we hardly ever discuss. I find all these solutions lacking. But what is the alternative? This system we have of loving people and then losing them, period, end of story, has nothing I can think of to recommend it.

Here is how cemetery trips go now: Both tiers of the George Washington Bridge are often choked with traffic, so the timing of the outing is critical. The Jersey side of the bridge spills on to many superhighways, which we maneuver with aplomb, barely glancing at the GPS. We drive past the malls, past Bloomingdales (where I always think about stopping but never do: a cemetery trip is very specifically a cemetery trip), past chain restaurants and tire stores and then more malls (and all the time I am restraining myself from casually remarking, *you know, this all used to be country*), until we see the diner on our right. Then we head straight down a suburban street—houses and strip malls—until we get to the cemetery. As long as we avoid the traffic, it's all pretty quick. Afterwards, we always eat lunch at the diner—a New York Greek extravaganza with a revolving mirrored display case of oversized pies, and a menu the size of, well, a revolving mirrored display case of oversized pies. Whether we are dazed with grief or enjoying the outing, we make our stop for omelettes, hamburgers, maltes, spinach pie, chicken soup.

Actually, the *enjoying the outing* part is a lie. Standing in front of my parents' graves, I always cry. It is always difficult for me to leave. I always have a terrible time pulling myself away. Maybe it's because I remember being in this place so many times with these very people. Maybe it's because their names are there on the stones. I know that, in the sense that they are anywhere, this is where they are—whatever bone or hair or fragment of cloth has remained—even though, every time I drive past the apartment building where my parents last lived, I crazily think that maybe if I just went inside and up the elevator to the top floor, they would open the apartment door with outstretched arms, my mother crouching down to catch my small children as they run toward her. (These "small children" now have children of their own.)

The cemetery is the only time when I am, in any sense, *with* them. I do not cry at the Barsky grave, although I also stand there for a long, long time, sometimes talking to my grandmother and my aunt in my head, bringing them up to date on family news. Maybe if I were to go visit my parents first, it would make it easier, because I could leave them to go see my grandmother. Maybe I will try that next time.

A few years after a burial, the casket gives way and the ground caves in. I'm not sure if the cemetery people fill in the space (given their history with the hedges, I am guessing not) or if, in time, the ground just evens out. I try not to think about what is actually there—dirt and rot and maybe skeletal bits that look nothing like the people who taught me how to hug. Even though I remember to come equipped with

Kleenex, I am always surprised at how I am overcome by tears.

I only make the trip every few years, both because it's a hike to get there from my home in Massachusetts (forget the fact that I find myself in New York several times a year), and because, let's be honest, it's a real downer, and I don't often feel like going through it. Still, I want to. I am drawn to it. I am drawn to the whole ritual—the bridge, the drive, the cemetery, the lunch.

Nice things I remember from cemetery trips: The time my daughter, around age four or five, visited my grandmother's grave (my daughter had been named for her). She was so excited to see that something about this person actually existed that she danced around singing, "This is Millie dead! This is Millie dead." I think my grandmother would have gotten a kick out of the scene; her ill-fitting false teeth would have clacked in enjoyment. And the time that daughter was grown up, and we came with her as well as with her boyfriend, who had grown up in Oregon. It turned out he has relatives buried a block or two from us (the Weinstein plot). They are now married. How convenient! They can make cemetery trips together.

And we have adopted Jennie Rackoff. She is a poor woman alone, her small footstone huddled against the hedges on the right-hand edge of the Weinstein plot. She has been there ever since I can remember. No one ever trims her grass. No one ever leaves a stone for her. But she is part of our visit. We brush the dead leaves from her plain, forlorn footstone. We feel sad for her having gotten marooned here, with only us for sporadic comfort. We feel good that we can, in some tiny way, make her feel better. We also know that this is insane, because Jennie Rackoff neither sees nor feels.

Still, her stand-alone grave shows how these burial decisions play out in ways we don't care to imagine. Families splinter, move, then re-group in new configurations. Only losers spend their time visiting family graves.

So what do you do if you are the one making this decision about where you, or your loved ones, will spend eternity? Hopefully you won't have to do it by yourself, in the middle of trauma, on the fly. My sense is that, even if you don't have a tremendous tie to a particular place, it's nice to maintain some kind of family togetherness, and you can define "family" any way you damn please. Strange advice coming from me, as you will find out further on. (Spoiler alert: my own personal future plans do not include New Jersey.)

When we were at the cemetery most recently, for the burial of my aunt Shirley, the Greek diner had gone out of business, which hitched up our distress level a good couple of notches. We thought that we would have to drive all the way back to Long Island before eating lunch, but my grieving uncle roused himself to announce that his little grandchildren needed to eat, so my cousin Googled "diner," and we formed a small three-car cortege and headed out through a flat sub-urban wasteland. The replacement diner was just awful, with a menu the size of a number nine envelope. We were the only people in the place. Some of us had omelettes, some had spaghetti. Shirley's little granddaughters, who were about five and seven, had flown in from California the day before. They were jetlagged and confused, but still darling. The lunch did help to move us out of cemetery mode and back into the world a little bit and, by the time we hugged good bye in the parking lot, we were feeling refreshed.

And so, if you asked me what I wished for most, for-getting for the moment about world peace or saving the planet, it would be that the Greek diner would open again, and we could spread out there—every last one of us—along the length of its opulent plastic banquettes.

DIVIDING *the* SPOILS:

I'LL TAKE *the* GUITAR

*T*HAT WINTER, A FEW MONTHS AFTER MITCH'S DEATH, my husband's uncle Marty fell forward, dead, at the kitchen table at breakfast one day. It was during a big snowstorm, so a whole day passed before his neighbors realized that no one had spoken to him for awhile. He was ninety-nine and lived alone, with a support system that, although minimal, prior to this incident, seemed to be working pretty well. Two months earlier, the family had thrown a big birthday party for him; there was no particular reason why we didn't wait for the one-hundredth, although, as it turned it, it was lucky we didn't. And of course you always think: Did he die because he had had the party and could let go, or are we just grubbing around for meaning in a case where the poor guy's decrepit muscles and misfiring neurons had no idea what the numbers on the calendars meant anyway?

Most ninety-nine-year-olds could not have mustered much of a crowd, but at the party, Marty's apartment had been standing room only, filled with neighbors, family, colleagues, friends. Marty had always been engaging. If there was a kid around, he would ask the youngster why he was involved with whatever it might be—a game, a TV show, an idea. "And what's special about that?" he would ask. He would listen carefully, then say, "uh huh, uh huh, uh huh," not passing judgment, but giving the child, and the idea, the benefit of the doubt. He was always sweeping his surroundings, looking for new information. He was whip-smart, charismatic, brimming with enthusiasms; but also acerbic, principled, full of righteous indignation when righteous indignation was what was called for, and sometimes when it wasn't.

Marty had married my husband Peter's aunt Leona when Peter was a child, in the fifties. It was a second marriage for both, and they had moved into the Riverside Drive apartment house in New York where Peter's family lived, and which itself could have passed for an extended family. The landlord lived in the building and, as apartments became vacant, they usually went to family or friends of the residents. When the mailman retired, the apartment house held a party for him. Because of the connectedness of the tenants, as well as their connections to the media, this party was written up in *The New York Times* as a local color story.

When Peter was growing up, he was always looking for people to take up some of the slack in the father department, and Marty was an obvious choice. He was much more worldly, not to mention more talkative, than Peter's perfectly nice but diffident father. Marty lived an engaged life—he was a talented musician and a natural raconteur with a wide social set—so Peter spent a fair amount of time hanging around their apartment.

Marty had finished college by nineteen, then devoted himself to the Communist Party. He was a schoolteacher and then, during World War II, a radioman, a job with one of the highest mortality rates in the service. The necessity of placing the radio on a high point made it and its operator easy targets. Marty figured out how to rig an antenna to the top of a tower so he could stay at the bottom, which significantly increased the odds of his survival. He made it through several big-name battles unscathed but, as a Communist, refused to accept any promotions. He explained away a Bronze Star, saying, "They gave it to the men who didn't run away." After the war ended, he was assigned to teach higher mathematics to officers. Back in civilian life, he returned to teaching high school physics until the loyalty oaths required during the McCarthy period forced him out. At work on the production line at Fisher Radio, he again refused advancement, so the owner, Avery Fisher, set him up in his own little engineering department.

When Marty and Leona married and moved to the Upper West Side, they switched their political allegiance to the Upper West Side Democratic Club. There were still meetings to attend, rallies to manage, petitions to circulate, letters to write. Once, when they were visiting us in Massachusetts and we had a school mailing to get out, they showed us the most efficient way to do it—overlap five envelopes with the glue flaps exposed, wet the envelopes with a damp sponge, then sit on the envelope pile to seal it while preparing the next line of five.

When the anti-Communist witch hunts went out of fashion, Marty went back to school, earning a Ph.D. in experimental physics at age sixty-two, and starting a new career teaching at the university level.

Marty and Leona knew people—jazz musicians, folkies, politicos, Upper West Side activists and kooks. Marty could drop names that were big in his circle (Billie Holiday, the Rosenthals) but he was just as happy spending time with people whose names would fall with a thud. Always, he kept an eye on elected officials, the people he called the higher-ups. I am guessing that not a single New York mayor during his long lifetime escaped his scrutiny or earned more than a C-minus in his book. The schools *should* be offering more to immigrant kids. The trash *should* be collected more efficiently. The city colleges *should* remain free. Marty was always looking for a good deal for the people; consequently he lived in a state of continual disappointment and hope.

But, if Marty and Leona could not exert their will on the wider world, they could control their friendships. They were always either going to visit somebody in Europe, or having somebody stay with them, for a night or a few months—their own low-budget international friendship society.

The high point of their social life was Sunday morning waffles, a fully-staged production, eaten on the oilcloth-covered table next to the window in the living room. Marty mixed the batter according to a recipe he was constantly revising, but which began with a sourdough starter that ran for years, as well as an assortment of grains, selected for taste and health benefits. The toppings included syrups that were gifts from their far-flung friends. The mechanics were jerry-rigged, with extension cords for the waffle iron and the coffee pot weaving around the philodendron, but the talk was serious and wide-ranging—movies, travels, politics at the level of the apartment house, the city, the country, the world. If you had nowhere better to go, the talk would continue for most of the afternoon.

When Leona got old, and a childish dottiness displaced the other parts of her personality, Marty didn't seem to notice. She developed a shuffling gait, was always saying, "Oh, Marty!" as if she were mock-criticizing him as if it were the old days and he had made a bad joke. But now she could not follow the conversation. "C'mon, Leona," he would say, taking her hand, leading her where she needed to go.

Caring for her became his next career. When she died of Alzheimer's he was lost, but continued his old disciplines: walking for miles up and down Broadway, stopping to chat with old friends and comrades, eating small healthy meals at neighborhood restaurants, working himself into a fit of exasperation at the latest instance of injustice or corruption he gleaned from the *Times*. The days of travel were gone, but he maintained their practice of sending out birthday cards to EVERYONE.

As Marty grew frail, Matthew, Marty's son from his first marriage, as well as various male cousins, began to pay some attention to his day-to-day and long-term prospects. It was very touching, because this role usually falls to women. They hired a social worker to come in once a week. The first thing that the social worker did was to get himself paid by the state instead of by the family. The second thing was to go through Marty's mail. Here is what he found: When Leona's parents had died, thirty years earlier, they had left Leona a bunch of stocks. But, because Leona and Marty did not believe in owning stock (the Communism thing), they never opened the monthly statements from the brokerage firm. Literally. So Marty, a man who had no problem living on his Social Security check in his rent-stabilized apartment, wearing clothing that gave palpitations to the hipsters in the now-upscale neighborhood, discovered that his accounts were in the high six figures. And so he began to share his windfall. The first recipient was Maria, the longtime once-weekly Mexican cleaning lady who, if we were being truthful, did not do all that much cleaning. But she was a reliable presence, and she cooked occasionally, and she chatted with Marty in the Spanish he had taught himself in order to talk to her and to her family—who had joined the circle of exotic friends and who, in the last years, were his primary care givers.

Also, with Marty alone and aging, Matthew began to show up at the occasional family gathering. He had shown up at the apartment as a child, visiting his father every other Sunday. Marty may have been a fascinating human being, but he hadn't been much of a father. His political life, his life with Leona, his Marty-centric life had come first. To give him credit, this was a time when fathers were not expected to have that much to do with their kids, and concepts like no-fault divorce or shared custody were unknown. In any case, it was not a surprise that, as an adult, Matthew had kept his distance. I had been part of the family for a good thirty years before I ever met him. He was a soft-spoken professor of an arcane area of mathematics who had a long white beard. It was Matthew who called Peter to say that Marty had died.

I could tell that Peter was upset because, after the phone call, he sat in his chair without moving or saying a word. I, annoyingly, tried to get him to talk, which he obviously had no interest in doing at that moment. Still, he was ready to drop everything and go down to the New York apartment to meet Matthew—to sit around, to decide what to do with the body, to arrange a funeral/memorial/whatever, to figure out what to do with all of the stuff.

But it looked like Matthew wanted no part of shared grieving, talking, planning, or cleaning. The body would be cremated; it was already gone. And although any number of people had keys to the apartment, he said that he did not want to enter it until he had the legal right to do so.

Armchair psychology will tell you that it can be harder to mourn when the relationship is unresolved. And I am guessing that this one was unresolved with a capital Un. Marty was fascinating, sure. But he had no sense of gratitude, for example. When he would come to your house for a few days, he would never say thank you for anything, despite the fact that you might have knocked yourself out picking him up at the train, cooking, arranging interesting expeditions all over the area, then getting him back to the train, the plane, or maybe lending him your car for an extended period. Any time he called you and you picked up the phone, he never said hello, this is Marty, how are you; he just started talking about whatever had prompted his call. He expected that you would recognize him.

So, when Marty died, Matthew's attitude seemed to be, let's just get rid of the whole damned thing. Let's take that apartment, which was lived in intensely for sixty years by people who prided themselves on not having, and therefore not spending, any money—the time-blackened floors, the dismal, splotchy walls, the semi-repaired cheap furniture, the layers of *tshatshkes*, not to mention what I am guessing were a lot of bad memories, and just make it all disappear.

I could hear Peter clocking in long phone conversations with Matthew, telling him that rituals were there for a reason; that he should take advantage of them; that this would make the family feel better and would help him later on. But Matthew wasn't buying it. He didn't want Peter to meet him in New York. He didn't want him, or anyone, to go with him when the body was cremated; he certainly didn't want a funeral and a burial. And Marty, naturally, had left no directive. When Leona had died, Marty had had her cremated. Although everyone concerned was at least nominally Jewish, people for whom cremation was a no-no, cremation seemed to be the default here.

A month or so after the death, Matthew called to say that he had the legal stuff sorted out, and would be coming to New York for the weekend. If Peter wanted to come and take something that reminded him of Marty, that would be okay, but he didn't want it to get more complicated than that. On Monday, a guy would be coming to clean the place out. Whatever "good stuff" was there should be left to make it worthwhile for the man who would also be dumping the junk.

Peter managed to convince Matthew to let the two other cousins who had been close to Marty come by as well. But that was as far as he could, or would, push.

Side note: a day after Marty had died, our daughter gave birth to a baby girl, also in New York. Peter and I drove in at the tail end of a snowstorm, and reached the hospital when the baby was an hour old.

So the plan was formed. We would come back this week-end. I would spend time with the new family; Peter would see them briefly, but would basically make himself available to Matthew. Our granddaughter would be around for a long,

long time. Marty-and-Leona-Land was about to disappear forever. Also, Marty-and-Leona-Land was Peter's last connection to the old apartment house. So it would be the last time that Peter would walk up the front steps of his childhood home.

There was also the matter of the guitar, one of two that sat on the buckling parquet floor under the grand piano in the living room. When Peter was a teenager, he had taken lessons in classical guitar, and he loved to play on this sweet instrument. It had been part of family gatherings, where the repertoire included songs of labor, civil rights, and the "folk" around the world. It was a lovely honey color, had a delicate shape and a soft, delicious sound. Also, Marty had told us, it had belonged to Malvina Reynolds, the 1950s folk icon, composer of songs like "Little Boxes" (made of ticky tack), "Turn Around," and "What Have They Done to the Rain." And guess what? My kids knew "Little Boxes," because it had recently been used as the theme song for a TV show.

I pushed Peter to ask Matthew if others could take something as well. How about a remembrance for our son, who was really taken with Marty's romantic, principled past? What about the other cousins and nieces and nephews? We'll see, Peter said. Peter was getting a lot out of being available to Matthew, advising Matthew, leading him through the stages of grief and family accountability, even if Matthew seemed to be a reluctant learner.

So Saturday and Saturday evening Peter spent at the apartment. On Sunday mid-day, I picked him up so that we could drive home. The city was clogged with old snow, some from a month earlier, when Marty had died. On the side streets, cars were encased in frozen slush.

In the apartment everything was a mess, with books, papers, pictures, files strewn all over the living room floor, piled on the sofa, the piano, the chairs. Matthew was walking around with a large roll of tape, packing up boxes. Out of the whole apartment, the only things he was taking were photos and slides. The great majority of those, I imagined, were from Marty and Leona's travels. Who would want to see zillions of pictures of European and American cities with unidentifiable "old friends," I wondered. But that was only my opinion.

As Peter, Matthew, Marty's nephew David and I took a break for lunch and the purchase of more boxes, schlepping through a freezing rain, I chatted up (badgered) Matthew. *How do your kids feel about this? Would they like anything of Marty's? Did you spend much time at the apartment when you were a kid? How old were you when your parents got divorced?*

"By the time my kids knew Marty, he was pretty old," he explained. And he reminded me that Marty's morning domestic routine was rigid, involving his breakfast and coffee and *New York Times*–reading, and bathroom needs. He had the leisure and the control over his time of someone who had not seen the inside of a factory in decades, and who had spent only a tiny portion of his life living with children.

Through all this, Matthew only referred to his father as "Marty;" never Dad, or my father, or anything personal. But here is what happened: by the end of the lunch, and the slushy walk over and back, I had decided that Matthew's approach was perfectly reasonable. *Enough with playing the grief Nazi. Give the guy a break.* His shared past with Marty had not been that great. Why give him a hard time about dumping it all?

Back in the apartment, Peter put together his stash: the guitar, a lot of jazz and folk lp's, a set of Paul Robeson 78s, as well as a couple of *tshatshkes* for his sister and cousin, and a Chinese silk picture for our son. Then, as we got ready to make long drive back to Massachusetts, I noticed that two very old large photos were still hanging in the foyer. These were genuine antique family pictures in their original darkened oak frames. I knew that the oval photo was Marty at about age four. He was wearing an adorable double-breasted topcoat, a hat with a brim and, amazingly, what looked like white leggings and white button-up shoes. Marty had told me that the photo was of him and, indeed, there was something in the face that looked familiar. The other one featured two young women in the upswept hair of the late nineteenth century. I didn't know who they were—some relatives of Marty's, I assumed, although it is possible that they were relatives of Leona's, and hence of Peter's. "Aren't you going to take these?" I asked.

Matthew was not interested. He had no idea who the two women were and, as for the photo of his father, he explained, "I understand the sentiment but that picture never spoke to me."

David, who came from Marty's side of the family, might have taken one of the photos, but he was going back to Philadelphia on a bus. Peter and I were the only ones with a car. I went to Marty's closet, took a worn, bleach-stained blue towel as well as a flannel sheet with big pink and white checks, and wrapped up the Marty photo. It felt too awful to just leave it behind. I considered taking the photo of the two women, just to save them from the fate of being totally forgotten but, because nobody knew who they were, and because the image didn't "speak" to me, and because the whole thing was beginning to feel creepy and sad by this time and I just wanted out of there myself, I left them. They are probably hanging on the wall of some jolly old-timey restaurant now.

In this case, perhaps because the one direct descendant of Marty's had little interest, and because there was nothing of great monetary value, there was no squabbling over the pickings. Obviously, that is not always the case. I have a cousin whose sister breezed into town at their mother's death, called up an antiques dealer and sold the whole contents of the house on the spot. The cousin who told this to me then had to go to the antiques man and buy back whatever she wanted. (Guess who isn't speaking to whom thirty years on.) Or how about my friend, another resident of Peter's childhood apartment house, whose brother, always a little bit shaky, really lost it when they were divvying up the goodies after their father's death. It didn't help that, because they were cleaning up the house to sell it, the friend had stashed some worthless dishes under the bed when it was time for the realtor to show the house, and then forgot to take the dishes out later. Her brother, who discovered the dishes under the bed, insisted it was all a plot to keep his inheritance from him. Another set of siblings who are no longer in contact.

Back at Marty's house, there was still one question to settle: Where was Leona, or, to be more accurate, whatever dust remained of her? When she had died, six or seven years earlier, Marty had had her cremated. What happened to the remains? "Oh," said Matthew, "Marty left them at the crematorium."

This was a jaw-dropper. He had left them there? Just left them? As in, on purpose? The answer appeared to be yes.

Still, the more I thought about it, the less strange it seemed. I mean, is it any more strange than putting the ashes in a vase on your mantel, or scattering them in the ocean, or burying them in the back yard, or digging a large hole and putting a body into it? In a certain light, all options can seem grisly or maudlin.

Another way to look at it: it had been years since Leona had died, and this was the first time the question had come up. She had not had children. She was old when she died; she had one remaining sibling, my father-in-law, who was also very old, and who had never been the type of guy who would wonder about where somebody's ashes got left. These people were first-generation Americans. They spent a lot of effort dumping Old World superstitions. And, what with the Depression, the Holocaust, World War II, and the McCarthy witch hunts with their anti-Semitic overtones, many of them had developed pretty thick skins. It was our generation, the next generation, the generation that grew up with more of a sense of plenty, that has had the luxury of being sentimental. We are more likely to think that those people have been too zealous in their housecleaning. Still, it seemed sad that the only residue of these complex and well-lived lives was a couple of cartons of low-cost mementos and some ashes left at a funeral home.

On the drive home, Peter and I re-told each other the still-amazing story of the small fortune. A piece of it would go to Maria, as Marty requested. The rest would go to Matthew, who was looking at college tuition bills for his own kids in the near future.

When Peter and I got home and unwrapped the photo of Marty, it immediately looked better, even just standing against a wall. In our spare, modern house it became an object that demanded attention, as opposed to being just one more crowded-in thing. I felt bad that we hadn't been more welcoming to those two immigrant Jewish women, whoever they were.

Since we have been home, Peter has been playing Marty's jazz records. He worries that he took too many "good ones," but he doesn't worry that much. He bought himself a book of guitar music and a sheet music stand. He figured out that his fancy leather chair works best for playing. The tone of the guitar is light and sweet, as I remember it from the old apartment. Peter's arthritic fingers are limiting his guitar-playing skills, but sitting in his leather chair with little boy Marty looking over his shoulder seems to make him feel good. Sometimes he plucks at remembered melodies. Other times he listens to bebop while he reads. Sometimes he just snoozes. This seems to be part of his remembering Marty—of keeping a little piece of the old days with him even while letting them go.

GRANDPARENTS GO FIRST:
MILLIE'S CHAISE LONGUE

*H*AVING SPENT A LOT OF TIME AS A FREELANCE writer, there is one thing I know for a fact: Everybody thinks their grandma is special. If not everybody, then at least enough everybodies that I have more than once run into the following directive in the guidelines for the "life story" features you find in the backs of magazines: No grandma stories.

Well, okay then! But this is my book, and so I can say, and not just in the back of the book either, that my grandma was special. Special! She was not just an outstanding grandmother but an outstanding human being, a model human being. At least she was those things for me.

The facts: Born in 1885 in Odessa, the cosmopolitan Black Sea port that was Russia's window to the outside world. The Yiddish saying, *to live like God in Odessa,* means to live a life of pleasure and prosperity. Odessa was one of the very few places in the Russian empire where this was semi-possible for Jews.

Her father was an *avocat*, she explained to me, which meant something like a lawyer, or as like one as a Jew could have been.

She had a Russian name, Miril, and a Yiddish name, Mirka, although I only knew her as Millie, the name she had picked up in London, where, at sixteen, she had traveled alone to join her older brother. There she studied dressmaking and became the foreman of a crew of dressmakers, but the story, told so much later, was that she didn't get along with her sister-in-law, and so she trooped off to Philadelphia, all by herself.

While I was writing this book, my London cousin told me that, in fact, it was Millie and her brother who did not get along. The cousin called Millie's brother, her own grandfather, a real bastard, and said that, after Millie decamped for the States, the sister-in-law sent her money.

When I knew her, half a century later, she could still put on British airs, sliding a regal accent over her Yiddish-inflected American English, straightening up and brightening up when presented with a proper tea. Unfortunately, she never fully mastered English, spoken or written; fortunately, she could laugh along with us at her bumbles. One night she promised us cherry ice cream for dessert, but we opened the container to find it was pistachio. Then we read the label: Louis Sherry Ice Cream.

When we began to frequent the Shanghai Restaurant on upper Broadway, I was shocked to realize that, in addition to English (sort of) and Yiddish, my grandmother was fluent in Russian. I had always known that she didn't like the Russians. I never knew that this had apparently caused her to maintain her own private blockade against the language. But speaking it with the Chinese who came from an area near the Russian border seemingly didn't count, probably like the pork dumplings we ate. (The Yiddish proverb runs, *If you're going to eat pork, let it be good and fat.*)

Oh goodness; it looks like the factual recitation is veering off-course, and we have not even gotten to the part where Millie tells me about her mother dying when she was only four, or recounts a wonderful childhood memory of washing her hair in fresh rainwater right from the barrel on her grandmother's farm.

Maybe let's try another approach: What did it feel like being with Grandma Millie? The answer would have to be: thrilling. Safe and cuddled and challenged and entranced by the fun stuff she was always in the middle of doing—rolling out strudel dough *thin thin thin*, making doll clothes from patterns she drew on smoothed-out grocery bags, fixing a lamp, painting paintings, sewing fancy aprons to sell to the neighbors, taking me along to meetings of her Jewish ladies' do-good groups, pretending to read me a picture book, as if her English reading skills were up to the task. The way she invited me to work with her let me feel okay about my limited child's skills.

If she was making pie, she showed me how to roll out dough which I patted into my own little pan. If she was cutting out a dress, she would show me how to make a pint-sized one for my doll. What type of dress, you ask? Oh, one copied from a picture in an old *Vogue* or *Harper's Bazaar*. She would draw the pattern, cut the fabric, carefully work the fit, and darned if the dress didn't look as good as the Vogue version, at least to my childish eyes.

Three pictures hung above her sewing machine. One was cut out of a newspaper, a trick shot of a black pug wearing huge glasses and dangling a cigarette in a holder from its puggish lips. The second was a 1920s sentimental illustration of a baby who had fallen asleep in the high chair—hair tousled, bottle cast aside. The third was a photographer's studio portrait of the family she had left behind—father, grandparents, cousins—all staring intently at the strangeness of the camera, seated with their hands on their thighs, except for the two young men standing behind, and the adorable little three-year-old girl in the white dress and high black boots, and the baby who could just about hold his head up. Much later I learned that the children, the parents of the adorable children, and the two young men were all killed during World War II.

When I was a child, those people looked so foreign to me, they could have been posing in a studio on the moon. Now, their outfits and poses and background still look exotic, but their eyes look familiar. I recognize them from my grandmother, mother, uncles, aunt, cousins. Those old Russians stare at me now as I write this. I took the photo to a conservator and paid good money to have it shored up, then put in a museum-quality frame. I even sent copies to my cousins. For a photo that's at least a hundred years old, it is doing quite well, and will probably outlast us all.

In the U.S., Millie married a fellow Russian Jew from a high-end family who had likewise come over on his own. As mentioned before, Charlie could never adapt to his immigrant status, and was forever doing things like going to the corner for a pack of cigarettes and disappearing for months to pursue some harebrained scheme. Or moving the family from rural outpost to city to city, one step ahead of his creditors. When, during Prohibition, he and an immigrant cousin who had settled in Canada established a nice little business moving liquor across the border, somehow the cousin, but not Charlie, ended up rich.

Through these dislocations and desertions, Millie, an extremely moral person, was left with four children, not to mention the debt. Through the Depression years, she sold Christmas trees on street corners, took in boarders and sewing, and took back her husband when he showed up, telling her children they had to show him respect. Admirable, but so nineteenth-century!

By the time that I knew her, Charlie was out of the picture, and her children, all successful, were totally devoted to each other, and to her. There were constant gatherings at her house, for a visit or a meal. But there was one given: In between the main course and the dessert, someone would notice that Millie was crying.

"What's the matter, Ma?"

"Nothing's the matter. I'm crying 'cause I'm happy. I'm just happy that we're all together."

Let's skip to my teenage years, when she was living with her daughter and son-in-law who had no children. By this time, the family had money, and Millie did not have to work any more. She fell in love with painting, carefully executing scenes from her travels, her childhood, her memories, her favorite postcards, using a thin brush and a very heavy hand on the oils.

I still loved spending time with her and, by this point, I was painting as well, another activity for us to share. But, as she would have taken pains to point out, a hobby is only a hobby. One day, she sat me down and told me about the pogroms—how, when she was a child, the Cossacks had come looking to kill Jews. They set the dogs on her uncle; she heard the screams while they hid in a barn. Then she perked up. "And that is why we have to treat everyone good. Everyone. All the time." The implication was that, if we personally did not maintain our humanity, lead by example, the world would descend into chaos.

That was the thing about Millie. She was all about making gorgeous and delicious things, but the things were kept in their place. It was the gesture, the moral, the human rule, that was important.

I think about this pogrom conversation a lot. She had never alluded to anything like this before. She was certainly deliberate about what she said, making sure I understood what she meant about good behavior saving the world. I can imagine that she bided her time, waiting to see when I would be old enough to take this all in. It was as if she had a frame of flashing lights that went on when she was about to teach you a lesson.

These were lessons that she practiced herself. Now that the family could afford a weekly cleaning lady, Millie would prepare a multi-course hot meal for the woman, and insist that she sit and eat it and rest a bit in the middle of the day.

One Saturday night when I was in high school and my parents were going to drive out to her house, I thought to myself: Saturday night, I don't have a date, it's pathetic. I'll just stay home. My grandmother got on the phone with me.

"I won't always be here," she said evenly, almost matter-of-factly. "We should spend time together while I am." Through the phone line, I could imagine the lights going *blink blink blink*.

I know that we two were extremely well-matched, that not all grandmothers fit the creative/moral/strong person mode, and not all kids respond well to it. My own mother, when she became a grandmother, was more of the Auntie Mame type, insisting that the kids call her Sally, whisking them off for day trips to the Bahamas. I'm not saying that the only good grandmother is a strudel-baking one, but that was the model that worked well for me. (Full disclosure: Millie's favorite TV show was wrestling; she cheered on the exaggeratedly savage-looking guys with their faux-savage names.)

When I was in college, I got word of the death of Ming, my grandmother's beloved prissy black pug. Ming hated going out in the rain, so Millie had made her boots that matched the flannel-lined black-and-red-checked wool coat with a generous collar that she had also sewn. If the thunderbolt grief that I felt could have been a dry run, I didn't want to know about it. By this time, my three other grandparents were dead, but Millie was the one that I cared about. I took the news about Ming and buried it deep.

The death of a pet is often our run-through on loss, hence the goody-two-shoes tone of children's books in which pets die. In the simplicity of the picture book world there is sadness, but always, neatly, a lesson learned.

My own son Eli, when he was five or so, produced a charming little backyard burial with his friend when the friend's grandfather died. They wrote notes to the grandpa and buried them in a shoebox in the garden. The friend's mom was a preschool teacher, and so the appropriate expression of appropriate emotion flowed across our adjoining Cambridge backyards.

But back when I was in my early twenties, things weren't so tidy in the feelings department. The first I heard about the impending disaster was when I came home with my boyfriend for a visit and my mother announced, "Your grandmother is not doing well." My mother, the nurse, usually so full of medical language, became tight-lipped. "Bad cough," she said. "Not getting better."

When we visited, Grandma was just sitting in a chair, not getting up, not offering platters of cut-up fruit, or making sure that everyone was seated in a chair that provided optimum comfort for that person's particular build. Always on the thin side, she looked scarily so. I must have blanched.

"Let's go for a walk." My mother shot me a significant nod. She held onto one arm, my boyfriend the other. I sobbed as we walked around and around the suburban block. "The sky is blue," my mother said. "See, there's a cloud. Here's a mailbox. A sidewalk. Dandelions." My family was not big on analyzing feelings, or admitting to anything negative. This strategy had served them well as they moved from being unmoored immigrants to becoming upstanding professionals. Why change things?

But I was at a different point in my lifetime, my first tear-your-heart-out death. At times like this, we watch how our parents, how our families, respond. We learn the ways our families "do" death. My mother kept her game face on, even as she took a leave from her job, moved into my grandmother's house, and dusted off her old nursing skills.

Spring turned to summer. I went to Europe with my

boyfriend—no itinerary, no address beyond the American Express office in Paris. It was the tumultuous summer of '68. We visited left-wing student leaders and upmarket squatters. Nobody talked about what would happen if Millie were to die while I was away. At Chartres Cathedral, I lit a candle for my grandmother who, I am pretty sure, would have fainted at the idea. But it made me feel better, so I told myself that it would be all right with her. When I came home, I was relieved to find that she was still alive.

A couple of months later, when she was obviously close to death, I came to New York for my filmmaking job; my boss and I spent a day pricing cameras. When I was done, I had a phone conversation with my father in which I did not ask him what was happening, and he did not tell me, although he did say that I should come straight home. I did not call my mother, who was living at my grandmother's. When I got to our house, my father said to his sister, over my head, in Yiddish, "She doesn't know." Of course I knew enough Yiddish to understand him very well. And I knew that, as much as he didn't want to tell me, I didn't want to hear. *Just get through it,* was my parents' mantra. *If you have to cry, go into the bedroom.*

Decades later, this all sounds convoluted, counterproductive, downright bizarre. Back then, I had the luxury of talking to a shrink once a week about my feelings, but I still had one foot in my parents' world.

Pretty much all I remember from the funeral is the rabbi making some remarks that I found politically offensive, about how he felt safer in Israel (continually at war) than in Detroit (where racially-based riots had raged that summer). Now, I'm not excusing his thinly-veiled racism, but really, given my despair and my difficulty expressing it, would I have accepted any remarks from anyone?

Some weeks later, we went to Bermuda on what I can only call a mourning vacation. My aunt and uncle, my parents, and I took walks, drank tea, and imitated my grandmother doing her King's English routine. This trip actually helped, and I am thinking that my family may have been on to something.

Several years passed. I got married. We had a baby boy. Then, in my second pregnancy, I thought about naming the child for my grandmother, if it was a girl. But what name to use? Millie just seemed old-fashioned. And it was difficult to imagine somebody else having that name. My aunt told me about Miril (ugly) and Mirka (weird, because that was what my family sometimes called me.) My stomach grew and grew.

One day, towards the end of my pregnancy, I felt slightly dizzy and heavy as a house. I spent the entire day on the couch, not moving an inch. I couldn't even imagine myself getting up. I felt that I would become one with the bumpy slipcover, the supportive foam. But here is what happened: I won't say I had a vision, or even a sense, but I had, all day, a feeling of my grandmother. It was the way I felt about her, the way I felt with her. It wasn't as if she was there; it wasn't as if I was even remembering her. It was just the Grandma feeling. And I knew that, even if Mirka was an odd name, if I had a girl, that's who she would be.

I am so thankful that my Mirka understood how having that name gave her a leg up in life; that there had been this other person Mirka, and that she was terrific and that I loved her so much. When Mirka was young, she kept a photo on her dresser. It was an oval professional picture of my grandmother

in her gray-haired years, rather tame. When Mirka was pregnant herself, waiting for her own daughter to be born, I emailed
her a copy of a graceful photo of the young Millie holding her
baby son in a long white dress. I have always found that photo
to be extremely comforting: Millie looks devoted and mater-
nal, and, when I was a child, I thought that the photo was of
my mother, not my grandmother. They looked so much alike
that it never occurred to me to think about who that baby in
the long white dress might have been. (It was my uncle Dave,
one of the first Americans to land at Hiroshima. It was at his
funeral half a century later that I wore my Eileen Fisher dress.
He has been dead now for years.)

Anyway, my Mirka, from a very early age, loved getting
dressed up, and was very concerned with the rights of others.
This was the entire comment of her fourth grade gym teacher:
"Mirka has a highly developed sense of social responsibility."
Say what? She grew up to be a social worker who dresses well
—a direct line from Millie. Of course my mother and I, who
came in between, also shared and passed along these traits.
But when a child carries an important name, you are always
looking for the pass-through.

One time, a friend and I organized a women's event at our
synagogue, a sort of reclaiming our past, or some such femi-
nist impulse. We decided that, because many of us had female
relatives whom we loved and missed, we would have a lunch-
eon. We set up tables of eight or ten, told people to bring in
photos and tell the stories they always wanted to tell.

It was way too successful. Nobody got beyond their first
story, their first person. Nobody wanted to stop when it was
somebody else's turn. And the intensity of the delivery! If

anyone could figure out how to commercialize that impulse, they could make a lot of money. I'm just saying . . .

So what remains of Millie for me? In some way, she is always around, a warm shawl on a cold day. Her cookie jar sits next to my stove. Theoretically, I share it with my sister—a few years at her house, a few years at mine. I pray she doesn't ask for her next turn. Two covered vegetable dishes, one gravy boat, one large serving platter, all in the peacock pattern— these I use every day. I used to have a bunch of the dinner plates, but they broke ages ago. I have some of her paintings in the attic, one in the house.

In my bedroom, her chaise longue has just been reupholstered again, this time in acid green velvet. I'm not sure that I think of it as hers any more. When it sat in her bedroom it had a skirt and was done up in apricot brocade, with two lace pillows. She thought it was the most elegant thing, bought at a yard sale and redone. She posed for a snapshot next to the chaise in a long dress, doing her haute-model pose: hips thrust forward, feet in a balletic fourth position. Okay, so she was in her eighties, barely five feet tall, and the dress was actually a cotton print. But she had the pose down cold.

When I inherited the chaise, years after she died, I removed the skirt, ditched the pillows, covered it in a deep brick velvet chevron print. Without the skirt, the lines were surprisingly modern. It became my husband Peter's favorite reading spot. After the print wore out, I went with a solid rosy chenille. Bad choice—it faded in the sun and didn't wear well. Now, the acid green really perks up the room. This is the third house of mine it has been in. I think of it as my chair, but I can always imagine her posing next to it.

I think about my grandmother in the way that I have learned that our brains work to consolidate memories. We take out a memory from long-term storage. We remember it, then put it back.

My grandmother's folded shadow is in my memory box. Every once in a while I take it out, reconsider. Is she as good as I recall? I treat myself to a little memory, and the answer is invariably yes. I was lucky to have had her. For me she was a respite, a role model, a strict and loving teacher, a fellow creative soul. She started out with a lot of advantages as well as a couple of tough breaks, had a trying adulthood, did a splendid job with the hand she was dealt. I can't exactly say that I miss her, since, in terms of my own life, she has been dead now for twice as long as she has been alive. But there is a place where she lives that produces a ping that is both happy and sad. And, as evidenced by the length of this chapter, I want to tell her story.

When my own children had grown up and I started looking wrinkly and gray, I really began to look forward to having grandchildren, because I knew how much you could love a grandma. As soon as my first grandchild was remotely capable of beating eggs in a bowl, I set her up with a whisk. Now, whenever I head for the kitchen, I hear my granddaughter's footsteps. "Tie my apron, Grandma," she says, dragging it behind her. "I can help." I also keep her in magic markers, poster paint, and glitter pens. We discuss colors together, the bright pink and orange that are her favorites now. We also discuss being fair to people, what is the right thing to do.

Whenever I get sick—a bad cold, anything—I think, I hope I don't die. I want to be with these little girls. Although my granddaughters would do fine without me, and although they each have another doting grandmother who does wonderful things with them that I would never do, I selfishly want to be their beloved Grandma.

It's not like I actually consult Millie on matters of morality or heart. It's more like a version of her is always somewhere close to me, standing ramrod-straight, all five feet of her, one leg shot forward in her model's pose.

Why We Mourn Celebrities:
Flowers *in* Their Plastic Shields

*A*FTER PRINCESS DIANA DIED, ON AUGUST 30, 1997, a grieving public piled flowers so high that they almost obscured the tall iron gates of Kensington Palace, her home. The same was true at St. James's Palace, where she lay in state, as well as at Buckingham Palace, the official residence of the Queen. Outside Kensington, the pile reached five feet high and, by September 10, the bottom had begun to compost. The estimate was that there were a million bouquets in that location alone, a nice round number, which means it is unlikely that anyone was slogging through the mess of rotting blooms, clicker in hand.

Her funeral on September 6, at Westminster Abbey, had drawn an estimated three million people, pretty much eclipsing the death of Mother Theresa the previous day. (Not to draw comparisons between the non-beautiful person who actually did a lot of good, and the elegant woman who—well, she also did a lot of good.) Scattered among the mountains of flowers, you could find an assortment of stuffed animals, which seem to have become a marker of early death. In the outpouring of grief for Diana, two separate incidents resulted in people doing jail time for stealing a fuzzy bear. Let's just say that emotions ran high.

People mourned for the beautiful, charismatic woman whose life was cut short. They could identify with the divorced mother with an eating disorder who had trouble with her in-laws and who, despite past disappointments, was still looking for love. They resonated with the attempt of a sheltered woman to do something useful out in the world. Also, her life choices opened fault lines in and beyond Britain. The running drama of her marriage became a rebuke of the old orthodoxies, even as her personal style displayed a more open approach.

That sense of being trapped, of trying to find and express her true self in a stifling environment, resonated with an awful lot of people. They had been rooting for her to get her life together—to find a place for herself, grow into herself, maybe move to New York. She exited her life dragging the monarchy into a slightly more contemporary posture.

So there were many reasons to mourn her passing. But still: In the four weeks after Diana's death, the suicide rate among British women ages twenty-five to forty-four years old rose by forty-five percent.

Those women experienced her death as a deeply personal loss. But despite what they, or we, thought, we did not really "know her." She was not really "ours." Unless we were the potential victims of land mines, her real life did not actually change our own. To contrast with two other examples of mega-mourning, she did not free the slaves like Lincoln or lift a nation out of the Great Depression like Roosevelt. But she did raise celebrity mourning to a new level. So really, what is the magnetic pull?

By definition, celebrities are out in the public space. We can see pictures of them. We can talk about them with our relatives and co-workers, with our closest friends, and with people we barely know. We can remember how they formed the backdrop of our lives, how they grew up and then aged along with us, all of which help us to measure the contours of our own lives. Looking forward, we can imagine how much thinner our lives will be without them. But most important is that they are available in the culture as objects of mourning.

Which our own dead are not. Our own dead have to fight for space to make themselves seen, heard, acknowledged.

Our culture is very secular, very do-it-yourself, very mingy when it comes to ritual. And if a culture is skimpy about those things, it is not going to leave a lot of space for the frankly depressing, unsexy way we feel in response to a death.

A part of this lack of ritual is just terrific. As a culture, we tend to have our eye on the next big thing, the main chance. We have an openness, a sense of anything being possible, a capacity to re-imagine our futures at the drop of a hat. We are not hemmed in by outmoded, rote ways of behaving. But if anything is possible, then everything is possible—and we can get overwhelmed. At the times when we are hurting, when we are flailing, we are less likely to know where to go, what to do. Having to make it up on the fly can be a burden all its own. We are shut off from the great sweep of human history, ignorant of the coping strategies our forbearers invented to get us through just such times. Social scientists talk about cultures being under-ritualized or over-ritualized, along with those, like the three bears, that get it just right. Guess which one we are?

We humans feel loss intensely, and mourning helps us feel better. In our endless quest to distinguish ourselves from other animals, one school of thought says that our species is the only one capable of mourning. But recent observation of elephants, victims of what can only be called an elephant genocide, have shown that, in fact, elephants do mourn. So much for our sense of superiority. But it speaks to how much importance we give to grief. Which makes it so troublesome when our culture shunts it aside.

So we do our best. We mourn in the spaces, small and inadequate though they may be, that are offered by the world we find ourselves in. We create ways to keep our dead front and center, where we sometimes need them. We take out ads in the newspaper on significant anniversaries. We erect "spontaneous shrines," the roadside markers where our loved ones died. We organize memorial runs. We endow scholarships. We put plaques on benches. We try.

Were things better in the good old days? Were our lives, and our deaths, more seamless when everyone in the village made the procession with the coffin from the church to the cemetery?

I am stuck on those images from mid-twentieth century Italian films. Lots of black dresses. Close-ups of the hands of old people, gnarled from honest toil. Glances exchanged between simple-but-ravishing twenty-year-olds. I may be exaggerating, but the forms are there for us to imagine.

These days, many of those forms are gone. Visiting hours? Nyet. Fixed interval between a death and a funeral? No. Standard form for funeral and burial? Very much in flux. Consensus about reasonable or proper times, places, occasions for displays of grief? As if.

I have so many objections to this, and some of them are purely grammatical. The less grammatically-obsessed among you might even call them rants. It kills me when I hear the phrases *grieving our dead*, or *grieving a loss*. Isn't there supposed to be a "for" in the equation? *Mourn*, I will give you. But *grieve*? Do it a favor. Keep the "for."

My next rant is about embarrassment. As in knowing what to do around a death. Here is the problem: Because we have so little consensus about what is appropriate or expected, we feel uncomfortable, and so we do—nothing. We don't write the card or make the call, or say, *I'm sorry*, when we see the bereaved. We don't ask, *how's it going?* weeks or months afterwards, or invite the survivor out to a movie, a drink, or a meal. We are more likely to stew in our own discomfort, as if that was most important, leaving the bereaved person one less place to turn.

It doesn't necessarily take much. (Not to mention the fact that the mourner may not want "too much.") What it does take is a public acknowledgement, a way to open the conversation, if a conversation is what the bereaved wants.

Right after the death of someone close to us, the change in our life may be the only thing we want to talk about. Or maybe we don't want to talk at all. Or maybe we want to talk about anything but . . . Whichever; it is the death that is setting the agenda. As time goes on, with any luck the loss generally recedes, although it pops back into focus both when we expect it and when we don't.

In some cultures, and in our own in past times, the custom is, or has been, to wear mourning clothes as a public announcement of a personal state. This can certainly get the conversation going! Some of us have a religious structure that's still in place: Jews and Catholics can fall back on ritual observances that combine honor and obligation. And Mexicans! They get the prize. Who wouldn't want a skull-shaped tattoo, face paint, pair of earrings, or sugar candy to mark the day, every year, when we remember our dead? But mostly, we are expected to mourn in private.

The one exception is our war dead. We continue an old custom of visiting military graves on Veterans Day or Memorial Day and leaving flowers to show we have been there. And throughout the year, we do visit a very few memorials—the Vietnam War Memorial in Washington, D.C. being the most powerful example—and confirm our connection to the lost. Whether we knew these people or not, we leave flowers, teddy bears, mementoes, which are then cleaned up overnight.

Detour alert: I want to talk a bit about cremation. In 1985, the U.S. rate was fifteen percent. In 2005, it was thirty-two percent. The estimate is that, by 2025, more than half our dead will be cremated. While I understand the reasons behind it— it's earth-friendly, and more in keeping with our values of individuality and portability, not to mention being less expensive—I just want to get off my chest the reasons that cremation strikes me as being sad. I probably would feel better if I could think about becoming one with the great nitrogen cycle, but I am stuck on the idea that we do it because we don't want our dead hanging around. Yes, I know that is unfair. Sometimes, by scattering or burying the ashes of a loved one in a favorite place, we sanctify an ordinary spot. Forever after, or as forever as these things get, we can enjoy the shelter of that tree, the swim in that bay, the gaze out over that ocean, knowing that, in some biological sense, our loved ones are near.

But very often, that's not how it works. I have a friend whose father's ashes are sitting on the mantle of his wife, the stepmother of my friend. Maybe not so bad, except that this woman has been remarried for a decade. Does my friend get dibs? Visitation rights? Some equitable fraction of the ashes for her own mantelpiece or place of her choice?

When we don't hold on to the ashes, but rather scatter them or bury them, it can look like the opposite, like we want to be done with that phase of our lives. (You can make the same argument for burial.) Either way, we have achieved that magic goal—closure.

And that, friend, is the cue for my third and biggest rant.

Whenever I hear the word *closure*, I think of a large industrial zipper. We heave up the pull tab and, zip! It is done. We are finished. We can go on. We have come to grips. Case closed. (Or, if you look into the derivation of the word, our grief is now enclosed.)

Which strikes me as being slightly insane. One, because that's not the way it works. And two, because that's not the way it ought to work. When someone is important to us, an intimate part of our lives, wouldn't it be weird if we could just snap our fingers and move on? Wouldn't that negate much of our past life? I am not saying that we should wallow in misery indefinitely. I'm saying that, in my experience, and in the experience of my friends (and really, do I need a broader sample than that?), our dead stay with us. They may not always be right next to us, pushing us off the bench, nudging us with their bony elbows, but they are somewhere in the vicinity. They appear in our dreams, we think we catch sight of them on the street, their voices are in our heads. And yes, I understand that you can go and visit the place where the cremated person has been buried or scattered. It's just that you don't hear about that. What you hear more often is the necessity for achieving closure. It's like the billboard ads with people with white liquid moustaches who are being asked, "Got milk?"

Yup, would be the correct answer, *I've got it. I'm done. I'm all closured up.*

Or it's a little bit like the plastic sheathing around the floral bouquets. Their purpose, from the florists' point of view, is to keep the flowers from drying out, which is supposed to extend their lives. But the effect of these wrapped items deposited on the floor, on the ground, lumped up, piled high, seems like a way to make things look good, keep things separate, negate biology, sanitize decay. But aren't flowers supposed to die? Isn't that why we offer them, because they are, for a time, beautiful and alive, but then they shrivel and die?

Plastic slipcovers have become such a trope for inauthenticity that I wonder why nobody has railed against those piles of plastic-covered flowers. So I am going to go out on a limb here, and say that that sort of public display of grief is a form of pernicious denial. I know that we can feel like we "knew" a public figure, and certainly the death of someone we had seen, if only from a distance, can be a stand-in for a period of our lives, or for our hopes or dreams. Still, much of the intense emotion expressed around the deaths of these public figures seems displaced.

The upside of this is the way that our collective grief can help to cement the community of grievers. As with friends and family, those who mourn together share an intense experience, strengthen a bond. The most extreme example of this might be Lenin's body, which has been on public view since his death in 1924. That old revolutionary is closing in on a century of being visibly dead. When the Soviet Union imploded in 1991, the president of its successor state, Russia, Boris Yeltsin, with the support of the reborn Russian Orthodox Church, was ready to stop bathing Lenin's body in the secret mixture and finally bury him next to his mother. But Yeltsin's successor, Vladimir Putin, put that change on hold. Although the government no longer funds the maintenance of the world's most public corpse, Putin's rationale was that, if Lenin were to be buried, it would imply that the Russian people had observed false values during the seventy years of Soviet rule. (Excuse me, but isn't that what the end of the Soviet Union was about?)

The people who wait on line to view an extraordinarily embalmed version of a Hero of the Revolution are not exactly mourning. But they are joined in a common experience of loss, a common reverence for what once was, and, in some weird way, is still.

We, however, do not have a Lenin equivalent. In our make-it-up-as-you-go society, we are thrown back on our own devices. No household altars to our ancestors. No All Saints or All Souls Day. No Day of the Dead. Our dead are in perpetual nighttime, out of sight.

But that is not how the human heart beats. We invent little ways to keep our dead with us. Because we need them. We need them so that we can remember. We need to use the strands of their lives to intertwine with our own as we continue, each day, to re-create our world.

LOSING *a* FRIEND:
GETTING *the* RETRO DRESS

ALTHOUGH ELLEN HAS BEEN DEAD FOR SEVERAL years now, here is what I still think about every summer: why couldn't the two of us just take one of our swims together in Long Pond? That was how we topped off every day that I visited her in Wellfleet, summer after summer after summer. Even if we were on our way back from the beach (long vistas, but not all that great for swimming), we would park along the side of the road, make our way down the loose dirt hillside, say hi to the thousand and one people that Ellen knew from the Upper West Side, and ease into the warm soft water beyond the lifeguard area.

Ellen would start out with a strong crawl paralleling the shore; I preferred breast stroke. But after our first spurt of distance, we would relax into an easy sidestroke. She led with her left arm, I led with my right. We did this so that we could swim and talk at the same time. We continued whatever conversation had been going on since we had staggered into her kitchen in the early morning—black coffee and some kind of protein leftover for Ellen, tea with milk and sweetener, toast and cheese for me—about what we were each in the process of becoming. We talked about jobs, creative projects, politics, kids, husbands, more politics. "But what am I supposed to do with this jam?" Ellen would ask, making a silly face as she held up a gift from some previous guest. We both knew that her domestic skills were minimal, and she could only face making order in the vacation house kitchen if I was with her.

The years and the decades flowed by. If I tell you that our friendship was like those swims, effortless and refreshing, you will probably think that I am glossing over the dark spots that can appear, even in a sunny clear lake. But here are two reasons why the friendship was mostly a smooth glide. Once we left college, we never lived in the same city. So we could be sounding boards for each other, waypoints as we constructed our lives, which always had some elements of overlap and some that were different. Luckily, we never lost our curiosity about what made the other one tick.

In high school, we had known each other, but were not really friends. She was more athletic (basketball and swim teams). Among the exuberant folk music kids who played their guitars and banjos in the quad after lunch, Ellen was the one most likely to throw back her head and laugh and sing, narrative songs with a punch and a beat: "If I Had A Hammer," "Wimoweh," "Wasn't That a Time." And me, the person who became a writer? Big surprise: I gravitated to the art room, the quieter kids.

But we did do college together, swept up in the civil rights movement. We thought about going down South to register voters (other young New York-area Jews got killed for doing just that) but we stayed up in Boston, where we were in school. We taught African American kids in ad hoc "freedom schools" the words to the Negro National Anthem, "Lift Every Voice and Sing." White girls could do this without irony at that period, and the two of us squeezed some time in, between classes and studying and fun, wrangling a room of squirming but earnest ten-year-olds.

One summer, a few kids from our college made what we called an Adventure Playground in Roxbury, Boston's African-American neighborhood. That meant hanging out on a vacant lot with whatever kids came by. We gave them tools, and together we cleaned out the trash, built climbing structures and places to just spend time. Although the others lived in rented apartments in Roxbury for the summer, I lived in an apartment in Cambridge, where I spent my mornings taking a course in color theory. (Cf. Ellen and Miriam; the same, yet different.)

At the end of the summer, Ellen said, "You know, Mir, I just don't want to leave those kids," so the two of us invented what we called a nursery school in a local community center. We scrounged toys we could use, I sewed curtains, and two mornings a week we schlepped in from our suburban campus, set everything up and then packed it all away.

I appreciated that Ellen was more outgoing. She appreciated something in me that she probably thought of as my being arty or classy. She had some kind of oral or food issue; she was the only person I knew who could eat and chew gum and smoke all at the same time. Although she was never fat, she needed some external structure around food. In college she was into Weight Watchers, so she was always counting points and making sure to eat a set number of meals a day. Her fallback meal was a large, mealy Delicious apple and a wedge of cheddar. She would cut the apple into chunks, and stuff them into her mouth, eating the pits and the roughage. She thought of me as being a gourmet, which I certainly was not, but which, compared to her, I was. (I liked to eat on nice plates, and was capable of cooking, and presenting, a meal.) At some point in the friendship I realized that her build (tall and large-boned) and her eyes (brown and deep-set) were like my mother's, which gave me a visceral feeling of all-right-ness. Ellen always had thin hair. By senior year, her wispy black curls barely covered her scalp. She tried a wig for a little while but soon decided: *fuck it; this is who I am.*

Ellen was a psych major, I was painting. At the time, I saw my creativity as a burden. Ellen's indifference to her visual universe may have been part of her appeal, the way she would surround herself with a jumble of what I thought of as dopey trinkets—dusty Mexican figurines, touristy Haitian paintings, origami cranes. In my surroundings, I was always worrying about color and form, but in Ellen's room, or later in her apartment, I looked past the piles of undifferentiated stuff. They were just Ellen. She had a long-term boyfriend, a lovely black man who lived in the projects in Cambridge and worked in a factory. We never told her parents, who were liberal but not that liberal. I had a series of weird boyfriends whom I do not want to discuss right now. After college, she went back to New York. I stayed on in Massachusetts.

A few years into our adult lives, Ellen's mother was dying of cancer. Her father had died a couple of years earlier. Mrs. Rafel was normally a cheerful woman, but she had never gotten over her husband's death, and she was looking forward to joining him.

I flew down one day to keep Ellen company. The hospice room was totally bare: just the hospital bed where her mother lay comatose, a couple of plastic chairs, fluorescent lights. All day we sat in those chairs. Ellen was much better than I was about keeping up the conversation with her mother, the kind of thing that tends to lag. I reported on my two little kids but, after a while, got stuck for things to say.

Finally it was time for me to leave. I leaned in close and said, "Good bye, Mrs. Rafel." A huge breathy shiver went all the way through her body. It was the only thing that had happened all day. Ellen and I stared at each other. It was surely just some autonomous-type thing, but it felt huge. When I got a phone call first thing the next morning, I knew that it would be Ellen telling me that her mother had died.

When Ellen first moved back to New York, she thought she would like urban planning, but soon realized that she was happy being a guidance counselor in the city public schools. She kept up with some of her kids for years, and she always had a guitar in her office; singing was the through line. When we were finishing college I thought I might like urban planning as well, but I worked first as a documentary filmmaker, and then as a journalist. In time, I got better at integrating the creativity/social conscience thing.

Ellen and I married men who emphasized our farther poles. Her husband Erwin was a Berlin-born Jew whose family made it out just in time. He was a music promoter, with tickets for all the best folk and ethnic music concerts in New York. But he was kind of odd—talking at you rather than with you, only sort of in control of his life. My husband Peter was ambitious and worldly in ways that they were not. Ellen and I each had two kids, although mine were older.

So, as things worked out, it was easy for Ellen and me to keep our friendship sort of exclusive: when we spent time together it was mostly just the two of us, although sometimes there would be a kid or two or a husband along. When my daughter grew up to be a social worker in New York, Ellen gave her lead after lead. My son, looking for a job in New York, made good use of Ellen's couch. But even on the Cape, Ellen's husband was busy promoting concerts, and the kids were in camp—or later, grown up—so the unit was most often the two of us.

Every once in a while Ellen would say, "I wonder how our kids from nursery school are doing?" or "What do you think we should be when we grow up?" Although by this time we were staggeringly responsible middle-aged people, there was always the feeling that we could change it all on a dime. Maybe Bobby Dylan *would* fall in love with me. Maybe Ellen *would* go off and work with Mother Theresa. I am thinking that, because our friendship had formed back when nothing was settled, we reminded each other of a sense of endless possibility.

Ellen's father had run a settlement house and camp, and a lot of this had rubbed off on her. Her apartment—tiny even by New York standards, but with a great panoramic terrace—was a haven for her kids' friends. One boy hung out there a lot: his mother spent most of his childhood in jail for a crime of conscience. Ellen raised money and helped out at a therapeutic village for kids who were developmentally disabled.

She "adopted" several old people in her neighborhood, partly because her kids had no actual grandparents, partly because that was who she was. Her friends were teachers and social workers, acquaintances from Overeaters Anonymous, which she had switched to after Weight Watchers. With their encouraging smiles and loose, flowy clothes, most would have fit right in to a Koren cartoon. At the same time, as the places where I lived got bigger and fancier, Ellen could totally get into my design-y head. (This sounds so shallow!)

She was always a big booster. She took the paintings of mine that I was ready to throw out when we finished college, and hung them in the hall of her apartment house. When I started making films and then writing books, she bragged about me to all of her friends. She always laughed as she introduced me: *My friend Miriam the film-maker.* Or, *My friend Miriam the au-thor.* Her enthusiasm helped me feel better about what sometimes felt like small accomplishments.

When my own mother died, it was Ellen who inherited the long sheepskin coat with the decorative patches. My mother was several inches taller than I; it never would have fit me. (And I never in a million years would have worn it, even if it had.) My sister, who was almost my mother's height, lived in temperate California. But Ellen had the height and the panache to wear that emblem of '80s haute-progressive style. She kept it for years, and she said she felt glamorous whenever she wore it.

The bad news came soon after my son Eli's wedding, an event at which Ellen had shone, with her sparkly scarf and non-matching earrings.

"Mir, I've got lung cancer, stage four. This really stinks."

But I was the one who couldn't breathe. How could this be? Ellen hadn't smoked since college, had taken up yoga, had continued to swim. My husband kept lecturing me about how I had to spend time with Ellen, spend *more* time with Ellen, but his well-meaning hectoring only made me mad. Ellen was *my* friend, and, if there was anything I knew, it was how to be friends with her. Well, of course that was bravado.

In the beginning Ellen said, "I don't know what I'm going to do." She said this on the phone, she said this as we took long walks around the city. She said this one day as I accompanied her to the lovely young Chinese woman herbal doctor who gave her the most disgusting brown sludge to drink. From there, we wandered around some more, until we noticed a small store on Eighth Avenue that sold Indian silks. Ellen chatted up the lady, and we bought a couple of bright scarves for her to tie around her head when she would start losing her hair. I began to take mental notes.

Because what Ellen was doing was brilliant. She remained every bit herself, but she turned herself into a mix of Zen and anti-Zen. She didn't particularly want to know the details of her illness. Biology? Feh. Prognosis? Who cares? But when she went to see her doctors, she brought along her team—her husband, her sister, her sister's lawyer husband—to do her note-taking.

She got thinner; her bones started showing. Her energy started to sag. At first she played her situation from both ends —as if life was still what it always had been, and as if she was living on borrowed time. But then, she changed her pension plan to have an earlier payout. She began cleaning out her nests—drawers full of song lyrics and school reports, then the dusty trinkets, the files and records and tapes and books and mimeographed sheets and sheet music. She was neither happy nor sad about this, it was more like, *this is what I'm into now, paring down, making smaller.* More and more of her life took on this quality of non-judgment, of being a tourist in a foreign land: *Here's an adventure. It's called lung cancer. It's called maybe I'm dying. It's called oh, my mouth has this lousy thing going on. It's called come and see me. Here's the phone number of a friend of mine who can talk to your daughter about being a mentor. Now I have to take a nap. Give me a hug. See you. Bye.*

She loosened up her rules about eating because, with chemo, she needed to keep up her weight. I saw her eat bread, pastries, maybe for the first time ever.

"You know how a lot of people, when they get diagnosed, they want to go to Paris or something?" she asked, one of the times we were hanging out in her living room, or enjoying the sun on her terrace, or eating in a neighborhood restaurant, or walking down Broadway, where she would be stopped every half block by someone who had to give her a hug. "That doesn't really do it for me. I guess what I care about is community."

Community she had in spades. In her world of teachers and social workers and activists, being supportive was the prize ticket, the gold coin.

I began to feel that Ellen was no longer just my oldest friend but also my teacher. The girl I remembered stuffing her mouth with unappealing apples was now sitting back, letting go.

Around this time, I was approaching my sixtieth birthday. My husband wanted me to have a big fancy shindig, but what I really wanted was something like the party that Ellen had thrown for her own sixtieth on her terrace—women friends wearing hats—before she got the diagnosis. But here was my problem: how would I face it if Ellen couldn't come?

Luckily, on the day, she felt okay enough to fly up. Ellen orchestrated a great trick to help everybody get to know each other. They had to stand in a circle around the dining room table in order of how long they had known me. I had specified no speeches. But Ellen announced, "I am Miriam's old friend, so I don't care if she gets mad at me. I'm going to say what I want." Oddly, I have no memory whatever of what she said. I only remember being beyond happy that she was there.

Ellen's friends organized a weekly sing at her house. Sometimes there would be a few people, sometimes a lot. Sometimes Ellen felt good; other times she just lay on the couch. There were Lance Armstrong-type plastic bracelets that said Ellen's Chorus. I thought about going, but I was always busy. And yes, I know that busy is a construct.

Let me just say here that Ellen had no interest in dying. She never reconciled herself to it. I find it hard to imagine how you would, unless you were in absolute pain and agony, or, if you were like Ellen's mother, looking forward to seeing a loved one again. Luckily, Judaism is flexible about these things. Whatever your inclination, you can find a tradition that supports your belief.

As Ellen spent more and more time on her couch, she became more and more Zen: *I'll try to come, and if I can't come, I'll imagine that I am there.* But one phone call was really scary. "Mir, last night I couldn't catch a breath. I don't want to die this way, drowning." I told her to call me any time, even in the middle of the night. What could I do from Massachusetts that her local friends and devoted family could not? I had no idea. I only knew that I could talk to her. I could be her old pal.

As Ellen got weaker, the chorus got stronger. Twenty, forty, sixty people would crowd into the tiny apartment and spill out onto the terrace, into the elevator hall, which was still decorated with my reject college paintings.

It became difficult for her to go out. For a while we had talked about going to our forty-fifth high school reunion; we had always gone to reunions together. Then we stopped talking about it. I couldn't think about going without her. I couldn't think about so many things.

The atmosphere around Ellen was becoming frantic. Her brother-in-law, an old college friend of ours, said, "This Ellen's Chorus business is getting out of hand. This week there were over a hundred people there. She should be spending time with old friends like you." I began to get a sense that every apartment house on the Upper West Side had an Ellen Club. And some of these club members did not even know that I was the founding member.

It was spring, two and a half years in. I was standing in my front yard when Ellen's sister called. "If you want to see her, you'd better come right now."

Ellen's tiny living room was packed with kids, neighbors, friends. They were whispering, crying, eating takeout food. Her son showed off his new tattoo: Ellen's Chorus. Ellen was in a coma, in a hospital bed where the couch had been. Her sister said she could still hear, but I didn't believe it, even as I remembered her mother. I took hold of Ellen's hand and told her I was there. No response. I remembered Ellen, saying to her mother in the quiet hospice room, "It's okay, Ma, you can let go." That seemed out of the question now. She was already halfway gone. There was no room to sit, to stand, to breathe. Eventually, I drove to my sister-in-law's in the suburbs to sleep.

When Ellen's sister called me early the next morning, Friday, I knew what had happened. I felt worn and shredded. My plan was to drive home to Massachusetts, then come back with my husband for the funeral on Sunday.

My kids, who both lived in New York at the time, told me that I was crazy. I think they were worrying that I would have an accident if I got into the car. It felt good that I had produced children who could think when I could not. They told me to take the train into the city and have lunch with them, and so I did. The three of us sat and sat and sat. In all the years I had known my children, *just sitting* had never been part of the equation. (Did I mention that my kids each had their own relationship with Ellen? That they were devastated by her death as well as worried about me?)

But here was the thing: the next night, Saturday night, the night before the funeral, was our high school reunion. I certainly couldn't go, but I sent word about what had happened. And here, if you will bear with me, I am going to take you on a little detour—a tour of the New York metropolitan area, and of the clothing part of my brain.

On Friday evening, my husband Peter drove down to his sister's house in Westchester where I was staying. He brought with him my sleeveless black dress with a ruffle on the bottom, and my strappy-but-low-heeled black sandals. I had not even taken them with me when I had driven down—what was it, only a day before? Not taking my funeral clothes was not like me. (See Chapter 1, "All Set for Black, Thanks.") I am obviously the type of person who worries about what they are going to wear, and who plans ahead. But I was so upset as I sped off to catch Ellen before she left me forever that I had left my funeral clothes at home. Or maybe, despite everything, I didn't want to admit, even to myself, that my attending a funeral was a possibility.

But now it was Saturday, and Peter and I were together in New York with a day to kill. He decided that what we had to do was to drive out to Queens (the far side of New York from Westchester) to check out a company that made Japanese rice paper shoji screens. He had been thinking about using some for doors in his office. Somewhere in the maze of numbered streets, avenues, and places of industrial Queens, my cellphone rang. It was Johnny, a high school classmate who I had not spoken to for maybe twenty or thirty years.

"Listen," he said, without preamble. "I just want you to know, you can do whatever you want. Maybe you don't want to come to the reunion, but if you wanted to, you could just come for fifteen minutes. You decide."

That made me feel so much better. I could imagine a way for me to go to the reunion, a way that would even make me want to go. It still felt too raw to share Ellen stories, but being in that old place, with those same faces (now wrinkled, but still recognizable), seemed like it might be a good idea. Also, by this time, high school reunions felt like the opposite of actual high school. People got together to repair wounds, to feel good about the others and about themselves, a massive group hug.

But I had nothing to wear. If I had not packed my funeral

clothes when I had hopped into my car, I had certainly not thought to bring a reunion outfit.

Still, what kind of person shows up to her high school reunion looking like she just stared death in the face? The subset of something charming to wear when you are in acute mourning is a particularly small one, and the fact that I am telling you about it at all no doubt reflects badly on me. But reader, you know what is coming: I bought a dress. In my defense, I will say that I accomplished the whole enterprise in fifteen minutes. As we drove back to Manhattan from Queens, Peter was able to sit in the car in front of the Soho Anthropologie while I ran in and looked for something that would, in some grim yet optimistic yet stylish way, fit the bill. I chose a retro cotton number with a full skirt. The colors, a persimmon and black print on a white background, are not ones that I would normally choose, but there was only so much time and energy I was prepared to devote to this endeavor.

Later on, I ripped off the tags and changed in the car. Peter dropped me off in Riverdale, the upper reaches of New York City, for the dinner part of the reunion, skipping the preliminary cocktails, tours, and schmoozing. It turned out to be a really good idea—lots of hugging, people talking about who had had crushes on whom, trying to fill people in on our whole adult lives in two minutes or less, and, for me, ricocheting between giddiness and sorrow. The next day, about twenty people from our high school class filled a couple of pews in the packed synagogue.

Later, in the blazing heat of the cemetery, it finally hit me how many people felt that Ellen had been important in their lives, how many people she belonged to. I realized that it had been years since she had asked, "What do you think we should do when we grow up?" She had become a better, clearer version of herself: not just Ellen, but really Ellen.

When I bought that retro dress, it wasn't like some tribute to Ellen, or even to how long we had known each other. Still, she would have "gotten" it, laughing as she followed my description of making our way through several boroughs, and of why I needed that dress. If the tables had been turned, she would have been fine with wearing whatever she happened to have with her (see the "fuck it" about her wispy hair). "Of course you would buy this dress!" she would have said. "This is just you." So what if I was vain, obsessed with how things looked? That person had always been just fine with Ellen, my old friend.

Organized Religion *and* Death:
What I Believe

*L*ET'S START BY SAYING THAT MY PARENTS MET OVER an operating table, slicing bodies open and then stitching them closed. My father was a physician, a general practitioner; my mother, an operating room nurse. In a modest way, they thought of themselves as scientists. Although their deepest impulses were caring ones, and although they were convinced of the importance of human touch, their training in the 1920s and '30s encouraged them to look to a future of scientific breakthroughs. When I remember them, though, I think of how comfortable they were with the physical. My father had a series of snapshots of himself as a medical student, smiling as he held his cadaver in a seated position so that he, too, could present for the camera. After half a century of doctoring, although he was thankful for each breakthrough, he was still convinced of the power of listening, of touching, of thinking and feeling. My mother was so great at giving sponge baths, at making a bed tray attractive, with a fine china cup and saucer for the soup, or a bright glass for the juice, that it was almost a pleasure to be sick.

So you may not be surprised when I tell you that, when we come to the subject of some kind of afterlife or spirit or soul, I believe in nothing. Or rather, I believe in nothing more than what I can see or touch. I am not the kind of person who looks at the intricacies of cell structure and finds the hand of God. Some of this is probably temperament, and some reflects the way I was raised.

My friend who takes her Christianity seriously is so disappointed that this is what I believe: like, how can I go on with my day, with my life, if this is all there is? And I do see how empty it must look to her. But to me it looks like the opposite—stuffed full to bursting. I am in awe of how intricate, and varied, are the ways that human beings have figured out how to live with the bounties and the constraints that we all face.

More to the point, it feels totally beyond me to understand it in any other way. This is how my worldview was formed, and I have never found a reason to change it. Santa Claus? Nyet. That was for the kids who weren't Jewish. (And yes, I know: Santa Claus is linked to Christianity by only the flimsiest of threads. But this is how the kids on our street when I was a child sorted themselves out.) Tooth Fairy? I think that early on we figured out that it was my mother who put the quarter under the pillow, which didn't make either the gesture or the quarter any less wonderful. And God, life after death, or any variation? As my father would have said, with a belly laugh, "Next thing you know, you'll be putting on *tfillin*," translated as phylacteries, as if that makes it clearer: two small leather boxes containing text, which are attached to leather straps, which Orthodox Jewish men put on their forehead and wrap on their arm every day to recite prayers. My father talked about *tfillin* with the same bemused tone he used for leeches or cupping.

Still, I know that there is a spectrum, that it doesn't have to be all or nothing. When my friend Mildred, another Jewish atheist, was dying, she decided that the spirit stayed on for several hours after the body gave out, and she wanted her family to sit with her for a while after she stopped breathing. They did, and they said that Mildred was right; they could feel her there in the room with them.

As I mentioned, when my friend Ellen's mother was on her death bed, she got a lot of comfort from the thought that she would soon be seeing her late husband. At the time, Ellen and I thought, well, if that makes you feel better, go right ahead. But when Ellen was looking death in the face herself, she started "exploring" the idea of an afterlife, although she didn't come to any conclusions. So who knows, maybe when I am at that point myself, I may change my mind. For now, though, this is it.

Still, I must add that the "this" includes a deep identification with Judaism. The religion, or, more correctly, I think, the way of life, is historically based on belief in a powerful God. But in the way it is practiced in the more liberal corners that I frequent, God, or, if you prefer, G–d, can be neatly side-stepped. I may be deluding myself here, given my background and personality, but in my spotty and self-interested understanding of my religion ("faith" doesn't really do it) Judaism is more about community, ethics, a way of living. In a sense, God or no God is beyond the point. The profession of faith consists of words that you say with the whole congregation, which works for me because nobody holds you personally to account. You are only accountable for your deeds. Actually, if you follow that logic, you are accountable to God for those deeds but, if you are like me, you kind of gloss over that part. So sue me.

Even if you don't believe the words, though, it is such a relief to have the words that you don't believe laid out for you to say. This is especially helpful if those words, those prayers, those melodies, have been said and chanted and sung by everyone in your family going back thousands of years, in my case through Russia and, presumably, back before that to *Eretz Israel*, the land of Israel—although, when my husband looks at my cheekbones and my squinty eyes, he always brings up the Mogul warriors. And both he and I have more blue-eyed blond genes between us than would lead us back along a strictly Semitic path, so who really knows.

I do believe, though, very strongly, in the power of ritual, those behaviors that get us across the edge zones between life and death. We need ways to say, *this moment matters*, just as it has mattered to people across so many places and times. And, in periods of crisis or transition, identifying with the community gives you ready access to the ritual. It is there, so it is expected. You have seen it done time after time. So when it is your turn, you have a set of behaviors that is available to you, neatly laid out in advance.

I understand that some people like to think of themselves as being modern, or creative, or not bound by stifling tradition. But that raises a major problem: at times of transition, of crisis, of exaltation or despair, you have to start from scratch, reinvent the wheel, solve the essential human problem for the zillionth time, learning nothing from the zillion-minus-one people who have solved that same problem before you. You have to do it alone.

So, if you find yourself in a community that has worked out its responses to these events over thousands of years, well, lucky for you! There's a business term that's popular these days—"best practices," i.e. a standard or a benchmark or a template—which gets at what I mean. You don't have to follow along blindly observing every tradition that anyone ever dreamed up, but it certainly makes your life easier to have a set of expectations and guidelines. You can sneak around them, rail against them, or ostentatiously ignore them, but they are there when you need them.

Gathering in a place, saying the same things at the same time, something flows through you. These things that you do and say create something that holds you in the now. The voices move in your throat. The ancient melodies echo through everyone you have ever known. You enact the ritual, and it nourishes you.

That is the visceral power of these rites, these acts. Jews talk about putting your feet in the path.

In my world, in the case of death, this is what that path would be: You bury the person within twenty-four hours, or a couple of days at the most. Cremation, embalming, are out of the question, because you don't do anything that would desecrate the body. After the burial, you observe *shiva* (seven days of mourning), in some sense. You stay home. You don't work.

People come to you to keep you company, to bring you food, to hold a prayer service each night. After that, except in the most egregious cases, long-planned celebrations continue. If, for example, a grandparent dies two weeks before a bar or bat mitzvah, life takes precedence over death. You recite *Kaddish*, a memorial prayer, every day for a year. Every year after that, on the anniversary of the person's death, you light a candle, recite a prayer. After a year, the family gets together for an "unveiling" of the new gravestone. At certain fixed times of the year, you communally recite memorial prayers, usually as part of other holiday services.

These guidelines or customs or rules, depending on your point of view, take the pressure off of the mourner at a time when the last thing the person needs is the pressure to figure out what they should be doing. They give a pace to the mourning, a social and psychic "place" for the grieving to happen. They give the mourner a public presence. They integrate private and public, feeling and appearance. They give death a place in the circle of life.

The clever thing about most Jewish rituals is that they are rooted in community. Honors are portioned out, giving many people real, or honorific, roles in the service. For key Jewish prayers, it is necessary to have ten men present. (All except the Orthodox now count women. Phew.) Rabbis are not necessary to lead services. It is the group of "lay people" or "civilians" that is.

I have seen how this structure strengthens us, shelters us, centers us, helps us to heal. Our secular culture has whittled away at our available responses to death. Just as, in our modern world, the actual death is most likely to happen out of sight, we are also expected to mourn privately and silently, the way we imagine those benighted Victorian women did, sniff-ling behind their veils. We can talk about sex all we want, but death is private, grief is hidden. In a world that celebrates the individual, this marks one more place where we're on our own, making it up as we go. Most pressing, we are expected to find "closure," like finding a magic ring that will make all the bad things go away.

Jewish practice gives us a different option. In this system, there are set times of the year to remember our dead—at home, and also in community. During Yom Kippur services, I know when this sequence of prayers is coming up, and I dread it every time, choking up before it even begins. The prayer book has versions of a memorial prayer for a mother, a father, a husband, etc., etc., etc.—even a convenient blank. There are prayers for our shared dead as well—a couple of famous rabbis, representative martyrs, and all the people killed in the Holocaust. It's gruesome, and some years, it just feels cruel to the reciters—like, *why are you making me go through this? It's a perfectly nice day outside, and now, for some cockamamie reason I cannot remember, you are going to make me cry.*

But it is cathartic; and it makes you feel close, for a moment, to the people that you once knew. Does it make for meaning? Does it take senseless deaths and give them the slightest toe tap toward sense? I wish I could be a little more positive in my answer. Still, if it does not produce meaning, at least it involves commemorating, witnessing. These people once lived. We (or someone) once cared about them. We still care enough, at the very least, to recite their names, to say, or think, or breathe, something of their stories. It gives our private dead and our shared dead a place in our history. It may not be much, but it is much more than nothing. In these small, repetitive, ritualized ways, we conspire to act as if our dead do not leave us; even as, by enacting these rituals, by opening ourselves up to memory and feeling, we do not leave them.

So community may be my belief. I am told that, in Alcoholics Anonymous, some people, who have trouble giving themselves over to the "higher power" that is essential to the organization understand "higher power" as community. That makes sense to me: that the strength resides in, indeed comes from, the entwined hearts of the group.

The stories we tell each other about the deaths in our own families are often riddled with inappropriate laughter. We are supposed to be solemn, distraught; instead, we break out in giggles or guffaws. A classic from the old Mary Tyler Moore TV show concerns the death of Chuckles the Clown, or rather the reaction to it. When the rest of the newsroom cast jokes about his ridiculous death (dressed in a peanut costume, he was "peeled" by a parade elephant), Good Girl Mary chides their lack of respect. But later, at the funeral, as the minister reminds them of some of Chuckles' characters, she cannot control her laughter. "Laugh, laugh," the minister tells her, insisting that she stand up in front of the crowd, at which point, she breaks down in tears.

Death and mourning are tough taskmasters, whipping us around in ways we may not appreciate, and certainly can't always control. That may be why we tell story after story about wakes and burials gone wrong—the corpse who suddenly springs to a sitting position in the middle of his wake, the coffin that insists on slipping down an icy hill, the man who finds that the gravediggers have dug the hole for his mother's coffin just slightly too small, so he has to jump up and down on it a couple of times to get it to squeeze in. I have a note I cannot remember writing that says simply *story about gravedigger and jackass*. Okay, let's imagine that one too.

To me, the idea of an afterlife looks like a vain attempt to have some control over a bad situation. However, I know how central this is to so many people and cultures, so I'll just let it, as it were, lie.

I know that I don't want to be forgotten. I know that eventually I will be. In Europe, where space is tight, after a few decades, graves are routinely dug up and the remains either buried deeper, to leave room for a new one on top, or the bones are placed in a communal ossuary.

So maybe that is the way in which we are all together. We hold on to some form of that wish for togetherness, because the worst thing that death does is to tear us apart.

What *to* Do *with* Inherited "Treasure":
Saving Just Enough *of the* Stuff

*M*Y SISTER'S SON WAS GETTING MARRIED AND, after only one totally depressing shopping excursion that my sister and I went on together, my sister struck out on her own and managed to find a dress that looked good, made her feel good, was bought at an outlet, and would probably work okay with the bridesmaids' dresses (fingers were crossed). The sales lady, who, my sister reported, "used to work bridal," suggested either silver jewelry or pearls.

Pearls! I had pearls. Many pearls. I had never worn any of them (pearls are so not in my vocabulary), but they have been sitting somewhere (in my jewelry box? my drawer? the safe deposit box?) for years and years, since the deaths of my grandmother, mother and two childless aunts.

The stuff left behind by the dead grows larger and larger, and I don't just mean the size or amount. Each individual piece grows in meaning, taking up more and more psychic space. It hardly matters whether you like it or not. It belonged to THEM, we think, and we need it, deserve it, or are at least obliged to conserve it.

Naturally there are variations in how, rationally, families handle the question of who gets what. In one family, after a death, each person got to write down two things that they wanted. Interestingly, these were mostly not the big ticket items, and there were enough favorites to go around. (Just in case, it might be helpful to agree on some principle of arbitration beforehand.) Some old people ask their offspring to let them know ahead of time. The mother of a friend of mine did this. All went well until, after her death, they turned over the requested items and found, as she had described, post-it notes on the bottoms. Except that the post-its were layers thick. Yet another family gathered for the reading of Aunt Gigi's will. Unfortunately, it was barely legible. What had begun as a neatly-typed document had been crossed out and scribbled over so many times that it was anyone's guess what Aunt Gigi actually meant to leave to whom.

But enough about them; let's get back to me, and the lead-up to my nephew's wedding. Most of the jewelry I inherited is pretty much worthless. But there were these pearls, the kind of things I am sure you are supposed to count as family heirlooms. How nice it would be for my sister to wear them, I thought. Maybe that would give her a boost as she stands at the seaside venue with her ex-husband, and her ex-husband's younger, more fashion-conscious wife . . . well, we're all grown ups here. I don't have to explain how life spools out.

In my drawer I found a couple of versions of pearls that looked like they would be suitable for a child—each option a single strand of very tiny yellowing pearls, totally useless for our purposes here. But then I saw a double-strand choker, good-sized pearls with a plain gold clasp.

Those would have been my grandmother's. And they would be perfect. I held them up to my neck and the thread, which had turned brown at the end, broke, and the pearls scattered all over the floor. The broken thread, the scattered jewels . . . spare me the haute symbolism.

So now what was I to do, pay good money to get them re-strung? And then they would be, what?—totally generic pearls (so out of date, so not like what we wear) that once belonged to a woman for whom they may or may not have been a big deal, a woman who understood both the draw of beautiful things and the absolute beside-the-point-ness of them.

And who knew if my sister even wanted them? But maybe someone else would want them one day. The next generation, my nieces and my daughter, all stand proudly at the *pearls— are you kidding?* end of the spectrum. But perhaps, by the time my own granddaughters grow up, fashions will have changed so much, or the pearls will have just become so very old, that they will once again be cool, or, at the very least, a remnant of a person so long dead, that somebody will want to put them in the back of her own drawer.

But, if we follow that line of reasoning, do we save every little thing? The three-foot-tall china dog that belonged to my aunt Jennie? My grandmother's cracked dish which I use to hold the sponge at the kitchen sink? (Okay, I like the colors, light blue and cream; so very cottage/early twentieth century. And, when I see it, I remember her kitchen, and her.) But what if I had never known her? Would I want to be lugging around a cracked old dish? How about a baggie of restringable pearls?

Our attic contains the very large paintings my grand-mother made when she was in her eighties. Why are they there? To be honest, because no one else wants them. It also holds the snare drum my husband took as a remembrance of his uncle Seymour. Do you know what I think of the snare drum, or what Peter thinks of the paintings? Of course you do.

The afghan, however, is another story. One summer, my grandmother had my sister and me crochet squares, each one a bright primary color. Our first attempts were dreadful, but eventually we improved. She evened up the squares, added a border, and lined the thing with soft blue wool cloth. The squares are wildly dissimilar, but it is still my nap covering of choice. Peter favors an afghan knitted by the psychoanalyst he saw during his teenage years (she crocheted while he free asso-ciated). But when we (or more likely our children) do our final housecleaning, I am guessing that those two afghans will be some of the first things to go.

But here comes an update: Universe calling! On the heels of the pearl question, I got an email. It seemed that my nephew was interested in using my mother's tablecloth for a *huppa* (wedding canopy). Both of my kids used the tablecloth when they got married; I sewed tabs on the corners to attach it to the poles. So by now it may be a Family Tradition, if not an actual heirloom. My nephew was marrying a non-Jew, so this may possibly be it for Jewish elements at his wedding. Did that make the tablecloth mean more to him than it meant to my kids (who both married Jews), or less?

My brain was whirring and, out of the blue, I was over-come with emotion.

Big problem: that tablecloth is so not my mother. Sure; the woman did cross-stitch it, following the printed-on pattern. She completed a bunch of projects like that—tablecloths, pillow cases—sitting with her legs up on the couch in the evening. She felt comfortable doing that kind of work because her own mother had been such a needleworky type.

But in terms of personality, this was atypical. "Your Gal Sal," as she always signed her letters, was effusive, ebullient, dramatic. She was definitely not handcrafty. But she was very organized and good at detail. She started out as an operating room nurse, and she always looked back on that job with nostalgia. Still—for her to be remembered as someone who dutifully jabbed her needle in and out, in and out? As she would have said, fixing you with a raised eyebrow stare, "You've *got* to be kidding."

It *is* sweet, the tablecloth-as-huppa conceit. I happen to know that it's a domesticated, feminized version of the older tradition of using a *tallis* (prayer shawl)—something that used to be used only by men. But in this case, was it only the *idea* of the kindly grandma fluttering, sheltering, over the heads of the bride and groom? Or was I just too cynical for my own good? My mother was so not the fluttering type. She was so ambivalent about so many things. And her frustrations, her dreams, her moments of rest with her feet up on the couch, squinting at her embroidery thread, they all came flooding back.

These women have been dead for, respectively, twenty and forty years, and now they came barreling back into our lives, elbowing the living out of their way with their pearls, their tablecloths, their faded scarves and their cracked dishes. *You thought you were having a wedding and not inviting us*, they hissed in our ears. They would not leave us; they scratched at our dreams.

Not that I wasn't happy to see them, as it were; I was. But we were not seeing *them* so much as glimpsing a strange shorthand version or prompt—Mommy who occasionally went in for needlepoint, Grandma who loved getting dressed up. I got the pearls restrung and even tried wearing them once. I found that they took on an ironic cast and, in addition, they held body heat, a comforting bonus.

Jesse could tell his fiancée: that tablecloth belonged to my Grandma. And she would think of that woman, if she thought of her at all, as the wrong kind of grandma—the cookie-baking kind, instead of the Bronx doctor's wife version of Auntie Mame.

Why did I care so much about whether we get the right version of Our Gal Sal? Because, being dead, the only version of her that would be present would be the one we constructed. I wanted to tell her about this upcoming wedding, and also to tell my grandmother, my father, and assorted uncles and aunts. But I couldn't figure out how to reach them, so I have just hung on to their stuff. I keep some fancy china pieces of my grandmother's in the living room, even though I don't much like them. I cook with my mother's spoon, using the same stirring motions.

My kids turned out well, I want to tell them. I wish you had been around to see them. And me? How did I turn out? The concept is too odd to process. The last time my grandmother saw me, I was just out of college and, as she might have said, a little *fattutst* ("undirected" might be a polite translation) a decade younger than my own kids are now. The last time my mother saw me I was in my early forties. I went by myself to visit her in Florida. One night, long after supper, I went for a swim in the pool behind her house. She sat in the dark and watched me swim laps in the warm condo pool. And I thought, first, that she must be getting old, to just sit and watch with no project she was doing, no jumping up to clean something, to offer to bring something, fix something.

The next thing I thought was that the only thing more boring than doing laps would be watching someone doing laps. And although I felt a bit bad about having her sitting there doing that boring nothing, it felt good to have her watch me. *No one in the world, except for my mother, would ever sit and watch me do laps,* I thought. A few weeks later, out of the blue, she had a massive heart attack and died.

Sometimes the only thing we can do is to iron the table-cloth for its next guest appearance, take the pearls out and get them restrung. Each piece of stuff becomes a talisman. It holds the void at bay. The pearls are nothing special in themselves, but one day someone might want them, and then they will be there—still warm, in a way, from my grandmother's touch.

How We Handle *a* Sudden Death:
Whiplash

ERE IS THE CREEPY THING ABOUT BEING A WRITER. While I have been working on these essays, I have been thinking: I wonder who will die during the time that I am writing this book. And the people I know who are likely to die—are they too ordinary, too confined to my own little sub-culture, not representative enough of the general population? Maybe I should, quick, make friends with some elderly sick people in Nevada, or in Amish country, so that I have a more general sample of the population. Enough with the east coast Jews and fellow travellers. And, most important, if I write well enough, will these dead people sell?

Those are the kinds of goofily manipulative thoughts that float through the waking minds and sleeping dreams of people who grind up their lives for fodder. They are the sorts of questions we analyze in writing groups, opine about over cups of caffeinated drinks, whine about on the phone to our writer friends. And then, whack, something happens, and you think: I was just kidding, God. I was really just kidding. Couldn't you have held off? Couldn't you have given me nothing to write about? Preferably a good long stretch of nothing?

One Saturday morning in late August, when Peter and I had been thoroughly enjoying the last of the clear summer days, I woke up after a good night's sleep, came downstairs and found him sitting out on the porch with his coffee, newspaper, and morning pills. Nothing unusual there. But when I started to speak, he cut me off.

"Sit down. I have very bad news."

"Tell me right away!"

"Werner died."

I brought my hands up to my face, and would not take them away.

"He fell off the roof."

My first thoughts were selfish. If you didn't count relatives, Werner was one of the people I have known the longest. He and his wife Patience have been continuous friends for my whole adult life. Werner may not have been my closest friend (okay, he was nowhere near to being my closest friend), but he was someone whose presence has always been a given, always a pleasure. And now, *bam*, just like that, no more. The possibility of his not being there had never occurred to me. It was only during that day of zombie-like wandering from room to room, when the gorgeous outdoors seemed totally out of bounds, that I realized how intertwined our lives had been. He was one of the few people who had been to my childhood home in the Bronx, for example. This felt like a case of: *from this moment on, nothing will be the same.*

The summer between college and film school, I had what would now be called an internship at the public television station in Boston. I was given to Werner. He was an endomorph—large-boned and even-tempered. He was also curious, observant, and extremely handy, with a love of tinkering, history, cars, architecture, and art. He was editing a film he had produced and shot about people who had not gone to college, but had done well for themselves anyway. I spent the summer with him in a dark air conditioned room, learning how to sync film (line up the sound and the image), keep track of tens of thousands of feet of footage, and shape it into a story with flow, pause, movement, coherence, punch. I learned that, even when you think you can't cut any more, you usually can. Eventually you will reach a point of ridiculousness, but it takes much longer to get there than you would think. I found that this lesson was just as valuable later on, when I switched over from film to words. *Kill your darlings,* aspiring writers are always instructed. But actually, you can kill a lot of both the phrases you love, and the ones that just seem serviceable, and your piece will be so much better.

The next year, after I finished film school, I was hired to take one of Werner's old jobs. Professionally, we lived in the same world, but our "real" lives meshed also because I loved Patience, the bubbly graphic designer by way of England and Canada, whom Werner had married just before that editing room summer. In those early years, I hung out at the house they were fixing up in Charlestown, the Boston neighborhood which at that point was still mostly townie and proud of it, with much slashing of newcomers' tires. But Werner and Patience were so genuinely friendly and outgoing, even though Werner wasn't particularly talkative, that they never had their tires slashed, and even became sort of bridge people.

That first house had four floors, with one room per story, so life in it was constant motion. Werner and Patience both kept their primary careers going while buying, fixing up, and selling houses, doing most of the work themselves. Werner had grown up on a chicken farm on Long Island. He had been told that he wasn't college material, I think because he was really good at making things. Now I am thinking, that's probably why he was interested in the topic of people who hadn't gone to college.

Fast forward a decade or so. Peter and I were renting Werner and Patience's charmingly patched-together vintage summer cottage on Queen Lake, a totally out-of-the-way spot in central Massachusetts. Their daughter was eight. Their son was four, just the same as my Eli. My daughter Mirka was a baby who watched the little boy hijinks with stunned amazement. Along with Henry, another film friend, we adults were shooting a PSA (public service announcement) on boat safety. Peter's friend Clark, who wrote the Charlie Brown musical, had composed the song for the spot:

> *When you go on your boat, please don't make one mistake.*
> *A ship without an anchor's like a car without a brake.*
> *And if you find you're heading faster*
> *Toward the brink of some disaster*
> *And your anchor's sitting back there on the sho—oooore.*
> *You can bet that you won't do it any mo—oooore.*
> *Without an anchor you should never leave the shore.*

(Clark died relatively young. This was particularly sad because, although he did not have any children, he was the surrogate father to his nephew. Clark's brother had also died young.)

One day, Werner and Patience told us that we had to come see a house in a nearby town they were thinking about —the Godzilla, or perhaps the Cinderella, of do-it-yourself dilapidated charm. They had found an entire Brigadoonish town—a twenty-minute drive in any direction through woods and sparsely-populated countryside before you could even buy a quart of milk.

In the early nineteenth century, the town of Royalston had been the summer home of the owners of the nearby mills. A grassy commons was surrounded by white-painted houses, most of which had stood empty for decades, because a wealthy woman had bought them up thinking that she would start a school. It never happened, and now she was selling the gem— the mansion at the head of the Common. We really did have to whack away the vines to see the thing—room after gene-rously-proportioned room with architectural details and some of the original interior painted decorations intact, plus deep porches, barns, fields, a woodlot, a pond. Every piece of it needed to be reinforced, replaced, re-done, except for the massive wood-burning furnace in the cellar, which, if you spent half your life throwing wood into it, kept the chill off a couple of the downstairs rooms.

It took a few years but eventually they moved in, although they always kept an apartment in Charlestown so they could scoot in to town when work (film, design, real estate) called.

Peter and I had an easy relationship with Werner and

Patience; it is rare to have two couples mesh. When our kids were little, weekends in Royalston were a major treat—one of the reasons being that, once we arrived, I could just let my kids loose. My Mirka was in little girl heaven tagging along with Emily, who was eight years older. Luckily, Emily thought that was fun. The boys would be out the door, collecting other boys for baseball, fishing, ice skating. (Now I am thinking: we didn't let them go ice skating by themselves, with no adult supervision, did we? Luckily, memory fails here, and the boys are still alive.) Werner would commandeer Peter, who was thrilled to hang sheetrock, cut trees, mess around with anti-quated tools, while Patience and I would cook, chat, visit, feed the pony. Sometimes I would go with Patience while she sang at the church next door. Always, there were neighbors stop-ping by.

Little by little, the inhabited parts of the house expanded. Patience's widowed father moved into the back wing. After he died, it became home to Werner's mother. After she died, our common friend Henry moved in, between wives.

To celebrate the millennium, they finished up the ball-room (yes, that was the second floor of the house). By New Year's Eve, the floor was only slightly tacky from the last coat of poly. It was a local band, pot luck, and a raucous mix of urbanites, back country folks, and creative types. Just this past fall they held a two-hundredth birthday party for the house—pot luck in the garden for well over a hundred, and a formal group photo.

After thirty years of work, the backyard was not only cleared, but featured a swimming pool, tennis court, and a formal garden whose fence they had painstakingly reproduced from old photos. If you squinted, things looked almost fancy, although the lady and lord of the manor were rarely without a potholder or a screwdriver.

So here is what happened: Werner had fallen off the roof, fixing a gutter. On the one hand, of course; where else would he be? On the other hand, wasn't he getting a little bit old for this sort of thing? On the third hand, you just wanted to shout, No! No! No!

Even when we yammer on about things like being careful, we don't want to really think about what can happen if we're not. Even if we know in our minds that anyone can be snatched away at any moment, when it happens, our hearts are broken, seemingly beyond repair. In this case, the four of us had gone from being twentysomethings to sixtysomethings together, sharing dinners and film shoots and massive house clean-ups and weddings and births. Why would we not go on forever? Even if we know that that is not how life works, it is impossible to imagine it, impossible to believe that this is how life *fails* to work. Would I never again be able to pick up the phone to have it answered by Werner's delighted "Meeerium!" before he handed it over to Patience?

Later in the day, I called the house, imagining the down-stairs hallway jammed with dazed people looking to give, and get, some bit of solace. I was shocked when the phone was answered by Patience, who sounded shaky.

"I am sooo sorry," I said. But she was one day further along on this terrible road. "We'll just have to learn how to get through it," she said, the English steely lilt taking over her voice. "I've never been through this before. There's so much to learn."

She began reeling off the plans in her small, slightly breathy voice: "We're going to have a celebration of Werner's life. On Tuesday. From two to four, in the back garden, because we don't know how many people will be there, and that would be what Werner would like. And people can go to work in the morning and come in the afternoon. Just finger food afterwards. If you bring something, bring finger food." Of course they would know how to organize an event for a crowd.

On the day, there was no question in my mind: I had to show up early. I needed to be there, for my own sake—to help carry tables and chairs, to see Patience and the kids and the friends, to gather as The Clan of Werner. Over time, they had done so much more than just fix up the house. They had the gift of really welcoming the rural types, the city types, and everyone in-between. But I couldn't help worrying. Their little empire had run on sweat equity, using Werner's unending patching, installing, and improving skills. What would happen to it now?

The first hint came when we saw their son Damon hauling tables and trash cans through Werner's jam-packed work room. We realized that we had become the old people; the ones with no energy who moved in a daze, who fell off ladders and roofs. Werner's death had come out of the blue. But now that we thought about it, it seemed like an omen, and it wasn't a good one for us. Still, if we were now incapable of action, it was reassuring that Damon was there lifting, schlepping, hauling, arranging. And Emily, as well as her husband, seemed to have the *keep the big event easy* gene.

On the beautiful late-summer day, the gathering had an odd sense of normalcy, with people happy to see each other even under terrible circumstances. The only ones wearing black were Emily's chic Boston friends, who cautiously poked their way through the grass in their high heels. Patience came downstairs in a plain black top, and a skirt with a Aztecy pattern with the colors she has always favored—black and red and white and yellow. "Werner bought it for me," she smiled. I wore a deep purple sleeveless cotton jersey dress, and carried plenty of Kleenex. I have been to enough funerals/celebrations/whatevers to know that having Kleenex is key. The men who cannot seem to cry may envy you your dripping tears or your sobbing, but there is no point in having to be wiping your face surreptitiously with your hands.

The tennis court was filled with rows of folding chairs. The flowers in the front looked like the standard florist assortments, not up to the usual off-handedly low-budget, elegant, do-it-yourself décor. The long folding tables began filling up with food. More and more people kept arriving. Services were postponed for an hour.

The M.C. was a man who used to be the minister at the church next door, where I had gone with Patience when she sang in the choir. But now he was finished with being a minister, and was wearing a Hawaiian shirt. His cheerleadery style made Peter and me uncomfortable; it felt more west coast megachurch than small-town New England. And the concept? I understood why you wouldn't want to be miserable if you didn't have to be, but we were here precisely because we *were* miserable. Where I come from, funerals and mourning tend to involve violent mood swings—laughing at inappropriate moments, crying in the middle of a funny story. This kind of event favored a more narrow slice of the emotional spectrum.

Patience welcomed everyone, said she was the luckiest woman in the world. She had been married to a wonderful man for forty-five years. Look at all they had done. And, glancing around the back garden, of course she was right.

The minister kept a tight lid on things. Three people spoke, with the tone tending toward rueful. He asked if more people wanted to speak. He called on two. And then he cut it off, just like that. My Kleenex never made it out of my bag.

Afterwards, we looked at the spot where Werner had fallen. To the right and left were spruce bushes, but he had probably fallen while moving from the roof to the ladder that had been placed on an old cement path leading to the street. He may have had an "event"—a heart attack or stroke, or he may have just smacked his head on the cement. There would be an autopsy, but there might not be a resolution.

Patience had heard the crash when she was in the dining room with a friend who was painting a mural around the walls. "It won't make a difference," she said about the autopsy. "He's dead. I know that. I was there."

On the drive home, Peter and I stopped for supper at the Colonial Inn, in Concord, where we had celebrated the first of our two weddings (long story). It was a reasonable place to stop, but we had passed lots of other reasonable places. I felt the need of someplace that would ground me. As our friend Henry had said, after the funeral, "I'm thinking a lot about the old days."

When these things happen, they jolt us out of our regular view of the world. We focus on both the loss and the person. We see the life of the person—the life we have shared— stretched out in a line. Their line has come to an end. A piece of ours has as well. As the Russian poet Yevgeny Yevtushenko wrote, "Not people die, but worlds die with them."

The next morning, I was off to New Orleans to babysit for my young grandchildren. I had long before promised my son and his wife that they could go away for a couple of nights. I was still feeling shaky, but my kids were solicitous, and the little ones of course needed attention, love, snacks, markers, clean underpants, meals, good night songs.

The next day, Thursday, after my son and his wife had left, I got an email from my English cousin: subject line, simply "Alex." The note said, "Alex has died today." I was wiped. He was, what, eighty-three or eighty-four, and had health problems, but still . . . This was not expected. He was a great guy. When we first met him, twenty years earlier, when he had married my cousin Monica, we had all loved him at once. And he had made Monica happy. I was still feeling off-kilter about Werner. This whole business was feeling really no good.

Peter called, wanting to know if I would fly to London for the funeral. What—from New Orleans, when I was on Grandma duty? Without my city cool weather funeral clothes? Given the constraints of Jewish burial practices, my trip would have to take place instantly, if not sooner. But the fact that Peter even asked shows how close I have felt to them.

That afternoon, another bad email: My friend Mitch's father Bernie had died the day before. Eight months earlier, Mitch's death was the shock that had started me off on this book. So that was the bad-things-come-in-threes. "Let's hope that this one counts," my son Eli emailed from his mini-vacation. Luckily, these three events started to feel progressively less tragic to me. Bernie had been old, deaf, depressed.

Certainly he had been in a bad place in the time since Mitch had died.

So this is what it feels like to be old, I thought. Before this, when friends or relatives of old people died, I used to think, oh, that's all right, they don't care; they're old. They must be accustomed to people dying. Sometimes, if the dead person was important to the old person, you would be reluctant to tell them about it, fearing that the bad news would send them off altogether. But—and maybe it's just wishful thinking—you said to yourself, oh, they're prepared for it; another person in their age group gone.

Sometimes that may be true. My friend's mother, who recently moved into a very upscale and appealing (*appealing*???) assisted living place, says that she is reluctant to make new friends there, because everyone keeps dying. I have not reached that place yet, literally or figuratively, but I am beginning to understand how I might get there. I have already gotten to the point where, as is obvious from my choice of subject matter in writing this book, funerals have become an important part of my social life. I judge them the way you might critique a wedding or bar mitzvah. How was the turnout? Was the ceremony heartfelt or blah? Did everyone do well with their parts? Did I get to see all of the people I wanted to? And was there enough parking?

I did make it to Mitch's father's funeral. It was just a week after Werner's. But whatever deity or spin of the dice controls the timing of these things was not done with me yet. That night, my sister called me to tell me that her recent ex-boyfriend died at age seventy. My sister called him a sociable hermit. He could be super social and charming. But obviously nuts. He was an old high school flame who had become isolated, so she brought him out to California to live with her. It went okay for awhile; then it didn't. She set him up in an apartment he could afford on his Social Security, and she remained his link to the world. After he died, his two sisters who lived in Europe said that whatever my sister wanted to do in terms of funeral, burial, etc., would be fine. So she had him cremated, no ceremony of any kind. She did discover that, because he had been in the military, he could go to a military cemetery. Afterwards, she sent out an email with a photo of him as a handsome, suave twentysomething.

When you write fiction (which I have tried and given up), killing off a character is all too often the cheapest of shots. What to do with the extraneous old boyfriend? How about the aged, despairing parent? Death sometimes starts a plot in motion (creating an opening, squabbling over inheritance, destabilizing relationships) but it is too often used as an easy out. But when all these deaths happen in real life? Let's just go with destabilizing.

For me, the bad emails did not stop. Luckily, the circles got wider, because the subject line announcing the next death that week included a first and last name. Joe Garland was a public figure in our world, a local journalist who trained himself to become a historian, writing appealing and densely-researched books about the quirky area where we live. For decades, though, he worked on a project closer to his heart. When he was in his eighties, he managed to bring it out. It was a brave and touchingly honest book about his World War II Infantry Division, laying out what life during wartime had really been like for him and his peers. Over the years I had interviewed him, had eaten dinner with him, but I was not his friend, thank God. Although his funeral would be a civic event, a way to honor a guy who had been an important voice of conscience in our city, there was no way I was going to go.

It is one thing to know that, in twenty or thirty years, pretty much everyone who is my age or older will be dead. A hundred years from now, pretty much everyone who is now living will be dead, even my darling little grandchildren. Even whatever darling little grandchildren are not even born. But that is no comfort at all when you get the phone call that pierces your heart, when you get the email whose subject line is Sad News, or Announcing the Death of, or even Werner Fell Off the Roof.

I don't have to worry about the deaths that come after my own. I only have to worry about the deaths that will hit me. If I look at family history, medical progress, etc. etc., it is highly unlikely that I will be alive thirty years from now. Or, if I am alive, I will be a mess, so why worry about how I will be feeling? Still, I will have to face many more deaths. But there's knowing and there's knowing.

Life is not always that great. We do not swan through the world. Our friends are sometimes disappointing. Our careers often are. On a day-to-day basis world events, local politics, bad weather, crazy relatives can get us down. But these friends, these careers, these sunny and rainy days are all that we have. Just these. And when a person goes, and we look at who they were, what they meant to us—well, they might not have been the greatest, but they were the greatest versions of themselves. Even if they were not so great, we learn something from that no-so-greatness about how we want to act, what we want to make of our chances. So, gone is gone. And we are still here.

After Werner died, I started spending more time with Patience. At first there was a sense of: *don't let her be alone*. But then we fell into an easy routine. It was convenient for me to come by on Wednesdays, the day she took care of her one-year-old grandson at the apartment in Charlestown. One of the nice things about getting old is that life can become deeply layered. When her living room floor was covered with bright plastic toys, I remembered hanging out with her when we were the moms, not the grandmothers. And one night, when we headed off to dinner and the movies in Cambridge, it was eerie how normal it all felt, as if we were in our twenties, and none of this (husbands, kids, houses, grandkids, careers, declining stamina) had ever happened.

Patience, I am happy to report, has been remarkably resilient. Having terrific kids, grandkids, and friends definitely helps. And, as she reminded me, when Werner was at the top of his filmmaking career, he would often be gone. Or maybe it's that she is an only child, and British. Or maybe it is just who she is. She tells me that one of their rental properties has been empty for a while, and that is worrying. But with old houses and young grandchildren, life barrels on. She is sometimes quieter than I remember her, but as she makes her weekly circuit between Charlestown and Royalston, she seems to be firmly where she is, neither in denial nor despair.

Postscript: Five months after the spate of summer deaths, my friend Ellen's husband Erwin died. I did travel down to New York for that funeral which, for me, was a heart-wrenching ripple moving out from Ellen's death. Then, the next weekend, we were back up at Werner and Patience's house for a party inaugurating the dining room murals that Patience and her friend had been working on when Werner had his accident. It was bittersweet: great to be in Royalston for a party again, and the murals were delightful. Deftly painted in a faux early-nineteenth century style with a very controlled, quiet palette, they covered the whole of the small dining room above the chair rail, and depicted places important to Werner and Patience. One wall was Charlestown, and featured the Bunker Hill monument, with people arriving in horse-drawn buggies. The wall over the fireplace depicted the Common as it might have looked when their house was built.

As friends and neighbors filled the large house, we could see how Werner and Patience had done something modest and yet grand. There were no more empty houses in Royalston. As they became available, some were bought by their friends, some by people who soon joined the friendship circle. They were never the aloof people in the big house; rather, they used the big house to center the small community, serving on committees and boards, opening the house to all comers again and again and again. The town still had no store, no nothing beyond the houses surrounding the small grass common, but now it was very much alive.

In the half-year since Werner died, along with getting the mural finished, Patience has spruced up the area off the kitchen which had been home to her father, then Werner's mother, then Henry. She says that maybe she will move in there one day, and her kids can take over the big part of the house.

How *to* Deliver Those Final Words: Best Eulogy Ever!

"According to most studies, people's number one fear is public speaking. Number two is death. Death is number two. Does that sound right? This means to the average person, if you go to a funeral, you're better off in the casket than doing the eulogy."
—Jerry Seinfeld

THE ONLY REASON I WAS NOT PARALYZED WITH nerves when I stood up as the only non-family member to deliver a eulogy at my friend Wendy's funeral was the fact that I was so undone by my friend Wendy's death that my normal speaking anxiety never had a chance to kick in. I looked around the synagogue audience like a pro, noting that it was standing-room only, with her son's entire high school class filling the aisles at the rear. I waited so long to make sure I was totally ready to begin that the rabbi, who was sitting to my left, and from whom I had learned this trick of not rushing yourself, caught my eye and frowned as if to say, *enough already with the prima donna. Let's get on with the show.*

Wendy was two months older than I was: fifty-one. We, along with our husbands, were the only New York City-bred Jews in our exquisitely WASP New England seaside town.

Within days of our arrival, a dozen years earlier, she had phoned me: "You're in the Temple!" (It was not in our little town, trust me, but in the neighboring small city.) "You moved here from Cambridge! You have *got* to come over right away!"

It was a friendship that was a no-brainer. And it barreled along without interruption until Wendy died of a quick-moving cancer, her bedroom full of friends who were singing, first hymns, then folk songs, then whatever came to mind. After she died, when her husband asked me if I would deliver a eulogy I was flattered, relieved to have a focus for my grief, anxious about the end product, excited to begin. At the time, I was working for our local newspaper chain, and was accustomed to writing on deadline in a newsroom with twenty desks lined up in rows. You had to block out ten other conversations as you conducted phone interviews or patched together, if not deathless, then at least serviceable, prose. So, sitting down at home at my own computer with only my husband, kids, dog and grieving friends to distract me was— oh my God, who am I kidding? It was agony.

Pretty much by definition, if you are asked to speak at a funeral or memorial it means you are hurting—aware in all your nerve endings of the void where the person in question used to be. And in this case there was also the twinning effect: Wendy and I had so many similarities. She was the first of my peers to die. I had been so intimately involved in her last year; when she took to her bed, it was my borrowed nightgown she was wearing. I missed her terribly already. Representing her many friends was a huge responsibility. And, to do justice to all of this, there was so little time.

Again: the situation here is different depending on your

tradition. For Jews, a day or so is about all the notice you get, unless you have the kind of situation where you are basically waiting for somebody to die, and your family is into advance planning. The benefit of the short lead time is that you get the rush of emotion, the sudden flashes of memories.

As a writer, I can tell you that this is not ideal. Academics have come up with something called the spacing effect that shows we learn things better if we extend our learning across time. As far as I know, no one has done related research about writing, which means that there is an opportunity for here somebody, but not me. I can only tell you that the more time you can wring out of your eulogy-writing assignment, the better the end product will be—more Kleenex extracted from pockets and purses, more nodding, teary smiles. Sure, that initial rush is great, but your talk will be vastly improved if you can let the thing marinate while you walk away, come back, walk away, come back. You will stand a better chance of getting the balance right, of putting yourself in the story (your relationship with the dead person is an important part of the reason you have been asked to do this) and then getting yourself out of it. You are there, at most, as an intro, a frame, a way to present part of that cubist view of a person who was, it almost goes without saying, different things to different people. (And may I repeat: this is not about you, although paradoxically, you can only do a good job if you enter into it through your own deepest self.)

And now, a plea to the people who are organizing the thing, whether funeral, celebration, memorial, remembrance: Give your speakers as much notice as possible. My worst experience along these lines was the time I was sitting at a relative's funeral and the rabbi, after the opening prayer, gave a run-through of who we would be hearing from. To my surprise, number four was me.

The first step is to just get down a lot of random notes, unrelated memories, fleeting impressions, philosophical musings, favorite phrases of the deceased. You basically want to follow the brilliant advice of Anne Lamott, the living patron saint of writers. Her breakthrough technique? "Shitty first drafts." At this point, nobody is judging you. Your first job is to just transfer as much stuff as possible from you to the page.

Another option is clustering, which its developer, Gabriele Rico, calls "a non-linear brainstorming process." In the center of a piece of paper, write the trait that you most associate with the person. Now free associate. Draw lines to other circles that contain notes about memories, images, particular anecdotes. In time, you will be able to shape these bubbles and sticks into sentences, anecdotes, paragraphs, meaning.

But here is a piece of real-life magic: as soon as you hear that someone has died, it becomes possible to picture that person distinctly. The extraneous stuff drops away, and there they are, reduced to their quintessential *themness*. This could not have happened last year or even yesterday. Even if you know that someone is on their death bed, even if they have lost all ability to communicate with you, they are still there. It is not until that moment when they are no longer "there," when they are not even "they," that you can begin to feel—*ah yes, that's who they are, who they were, who they will always be*. It's like they have a Miss America-type banner across their middle, saying something like Great Friend, or The Person Who

Taught Me How to Swim (if you're lucky they taught you that thing, whatever it was, both literally and figuratively) or The Pearl Mesta of Avon Hill, or Last of His Generation, or Some People Know How to Have a Good Time.

Particularly if you are in charge, or have been asked to give a definitive speech, and not just your personal remembrances, you need to do a little reality check. Find out the actual life situation of the dearly departed, and make sure you get it right. A friend of mine who is a rabbi told me about one memorable funeral he performed. At his meeting with the family beforehand, they told him the outline of the man's life —widowed, lots of illness, estranged from his children. Easy, my friend thought; I'll talk about Job.

But, at the end of the funeral, as he was walking out behind the coffin, reciting the twenty-third psalm, someone yelled out, "A wife counts for nothing?" The rabbi kept on reading and walking. She came up next to him; yelled her question louder. They were almost at the door. When they got outside, he found the family, who admitted, "Yeah; she was married to him for twenty-five years. She took care of him, but we never liked her."

And here is something I learned through years of daily journalism. It is close to impossible to be too obvious or sound too dumb. You are the stand-in for the audience wanting to know: What? Really? Huh? Being specific is your best bet. How did the person look, act, think, sound? What is the strongest image you have of them? What were they typically doing? What did they do with you, or you with them? What is the hole that has suddenly opened up in the world? And (just open up a vein here) how did they make you feel?

For Wendy, I told how, after that initial phone call, I came over with my kids to what turned out to be "this palatial spread—fairytale house, green sloping lawns, an ocean—the works.

"But Wendy did not live any fairytale life. She was most at home in a world of eccentrics, artists, and oddballs. Traveling in the realms of the rich and the semi-famous was often a stretch. We'd be on some sailboat in Maine, or some ski lift in Utah, and Wendy's take on the scene often carried with it a whiff of the Lower East Side.

"Wendy was a stalker after transcendent experiences, aesthetic highs. She lived in her body, most often amazed and enthralled. Every person she met was brilliant! A genius! Every book she read, every play or dance performance: Amazing! Fantastic!

"And if she arrived late, disheveled, head still wet from her swim, well, what the hell; when she was with you, she was: Excited! Expectant! *On*."

And here we come to the elephant in the room. The reason that Wendy lived in a fairytale mansion was that her husband, who also came from humble circumstances, was a brilliant guy who made a ton of money and bought a big place and got to hang out with interesting people. But he was a difficult person, and their marriage contained long periods of the two of them not speaking to each other, as well as other things I don't want to go into. (He is dead now also.) Every time a new purchase would enter their world Wendy would say, "One more thing to feel embarrassed about."

I alluded to this in a gentle way, saying that, for example, "When we went on our walks together, Wendy used to complain about Bernie . . ." or that, over the year of the cancer, "Bernie became a person transformed." The people who knew the real story knew that I wasn't ignoring the elephant, but I only showed, as it were, the tip of the trunk. Each case is different, and you will have to decide how to refer to that pachyderm.

Humor can help here, but obviously, I am pushing you in the direction of: *We are all human. It is the way we deal with our all-too-human frailties that allows us to become who we are.* Nobody would mourn a stick figure. Real human beings, whether lovable, laughable or barely bearable, are the best we've got. And the obverse is, strangely, when we're toting up the pluses and minuses, we sometimes find that the most flawed people are the ones who might just remind us of saints.

There is a Jewish legend that might be helpful here. *Lamed vovniks* are thirty-six righteous people who live in the world at any one time. They are always being born, always living, always dying. They don't know each other, and they may not even know that they are *lamed vovniks*. (The name comes from the Hebrew letters that correspond to thirty and six.) They are extraordinary people, but they pass unnoticed. It is for the sake of these people that God does not destroy the world.

It is a reasonable exercise, when writing a eulogy, to consider whether the person you are writing about could possibly be one of the *lamed vovniks*. And no, I have not lost my marbles. It is just a way of getting past the imperfectness of every living being, and seeing flawed humans in all their idiosyncratic perfection.

Wendy could be intensely frustrating. We worked together on a women's publication which, as I said in the eulogy, "mostly meant getting her to try to hunt down some of the scraps of paper on which she had scribbled the phone numbers of people to whom she was supposed to be selling ads when she wasn't busy fixing them up." See what I mean about being specific?

A plus is if we can come out of the experience with a Lesson Learned: if this person's life can be neatened up or boiled down to something we can take away with us. Whatever it is, it's best to say it plain and unadorned. We live in a time that is suspicious of rhetoric, allergic to hyperbole. So just give it to us straight. *This man not only knew his limits but reveled in them. That woman would do anything for the cause she believed in. This person, when she knew she was dying, realized that in fact, she had no desire to go to Paris; she only wanted to hang out with her friends.*

For Wendy I wrote about how everything changed when she got the diagnosis.

"Her first reaction was, 'That's like totally bullshit; it's like so ridiculous!' But she marshaled herself for the fight. She grew vegetables, upped her exercise program, hunted down every guru and healer she could find. She had the Tibetan monk chanting in the living room; she set up the gospel choir to sing in Bernie's office. She tried the acupuncturist, the masseuse, the Chinese herbalist, not to mention the massed forces of modern medicine. She never accepted the cancer. And I mean, never.

"In this awful year, Wendy came into her own, took her life confidently in her own hands. A couple of days ago, she even mastered the art of holding court. She refused to admit that she was dying, but she shooed the extra people out of the room so she could have time alone with every one who was there.

"No more being late, or frazzled. No more rushing in from the pool, the kids' school, the concert, the job. Wendy, for one week of her life, stayed still.

"If cancer and an early death weren't such tragedies, they would have been a blessing, maybe even a miracle. This past year Wendy was finally able to jettison the details of daily living that could be her downfall. She lived in the moment, communed with her old friends and with the people she'd just picked up on her travels, performed her totally Wendy-esque dance of life."

So here is my advice for actually delivering the speech: Make an extra copy, and give it to somebody to hold. With all the emotional pinballs careening around, there is a better-than-average chance that you will forget your paper or lose it en route. And a little trick for stage fright: As you walk up to the podium, clench your hands into fists. (What if you are carrying your speech? Slide it under one arm, or just do this exercise with one fist. But it works better with two.) Squeeze so tightly that you feel your nails digging into your palms. You will feel a tingle throughout your body. As you get to the podium, let your hands go. Now you will get a rush of relief. Magic! You are good to go.

So now you are up there. Take a moment to calm yourself before you begin. Then, speak slowly, clearly, and with appropriate volume. Look up from your notes or your speech as often as you can, and look at the people in the audience. Every once in a while, address the back of the room. Now, re-read that last bit of advice and exaggerate it. Speak more slowly, more clearly and more loudly than you think is normal. The audience will appreciate this. It will slow down their heartbeats, as well as yours. It will set the tone, giving them space to remember, to think, and to feel.

In the interests of decency, I must tell you that some people need just the opposite. My friend Sally is a self-described weeper. "As long as my eyes are on my-friends-the-words I'm fine. If I look up and see everyone just looking at me with loving compassion, I lose it." She worries about the tears filling up her glasses. She worries about the audience getting uncomfortable watching her crying.

Or you may not want to speak at all. Most often, spouses don't speak—I am guessing because they are just too overcome. As Sally put it when she was remembering her husband's memorial, at which she stayed seated: "I didn't want to be brave." And if you want to stand up there with your spouse or your sibling or your friend while they read the words you are unable to say out loud, feel free.

If you do speak, unless you know you are a weeper, like Sally, I recommend getting your head up from the page. If you are overcome by grief just stop, stand still, look down if that helps you, and breathe. If you are crying, then let yourself cry. You may not think it will ever stop, but it will. Eventually (and it will be sooner than you think) you will pull yourself together, and you will go on. Everyone will feel great empathy and respect for you for having brought yourself back from the public brink. It's just one of those little card tricks we learn as adults.

What kind of eulogy would I like to have? Of course there

are specific traits I hope my children and friends will include, but most likely my little vanities will go unnoticed. (I expect that my husband will be too distraught to speak.) The touching thing about having people say nice things about you is the way you are surprised by what they remember, what they think is important, which is one of the reasons people say what a shame it is we can't be at our own funerals. When my daughter was in kindergarten, her teacher had the kids dictate Mothers Day cards, complete with ill-formed letters and gloppy glitter. My daughter's said, "I love my mommy because she makes me cocoa. On long trips, she lets me sleep in the car." That was really funny because, as any parent knows, on long trips you are desperate to have your child go to sleep and leave you in peace for a while to contemplate the blessed boredom of the road ahead. But she remembered it as a favor I did for her, something that made her feel good.

Especially when people eulogize a parent or grandparent, they talk about the particular thing they customarily did together—fishing or playing the penny slots or going out for donuts. It tends to be something supremely ordinary, the equivalent of napping in the car, but it's the doing it together that counts. I talked about skiing with Wendy. She was a beautiful skier, much better than I was. One time we worked up our courage to try a hill that was steep and narrow. After we negotiated it successfully she said, "Let's try OUR little run again. I think we can do it. Let's go back to our hill." Not only do I still think of that run as OUR hill, but I still think of Wendy as the person who taught me that concept, of taking bits of the world and claiming ownership—not for yourself, but to be shared with the people you love.

When you are delivering a eulogy, standing up in front of all those people, you are alone. But not really. Because, at this permeable moment, when the subject of your talk is moving from being available to being available only in memory, you are there to channel him or her, to keep your loved one, in some way, alive.

Here is how I ended Wendy's eulogy: "Well, Wendy, it's, like, total bullshit that you're dead. You were brilliant; you were a genius. And it was, like, totally fantastic being your friend."

ONE WAY TRIP:

THE LIGHTS ARE *on* TIMERS;

EVENTUALLY THEY GO OUT

*T*HE FAMILY HAS ONE OF THE ICONIC AMERICAN names. It, meaning a series of trusts, owns a piece of land so naturally beautiful, so artfully maintained, so purposefully remote as to provoke fevers. But don't start taking your aspirin yet. It is highly unlikely that you will ever get to see it. I was able to visit only because of a connection to someone who has a connection.

The landscape is dotted with vacation houses, cottages, scenic outbuildings, appropriate animals. Off a dirt path sits an old barn with weathered shingle siding, blocky and plain. This family is so established that the last thing they have to worry about is impressing anybody. And unprepossessing is itself a formidable style.

When you open the door and climb up the unpainted wooden steps, you find what might be the ultimate in low-key one-upsmanship or self-confident genealogy—a barn-sized room dedicated to nothing except the unfolding of the family.

The saga begins with 8"x12" pictures of the progenitor and his wife, showing names, dates of birth, marriage, death. Their children progress in neat lines around the walls of the room. Then, on each section of wall, the generations—one, two, three, four, five, six, seven, eight, nine, ten—make their way down the walls as people continue to be born, and to die.

Each line of the family has its own shade of thin tape connecting color-coordinated small squares of file card paper on which are typewritten individual names. Marriages, divorces, dates of birth and death: these are the plainest of facts, tacked onto white-painted sheets of homasote. Hundreds of names, a few of them quite famous. No details beyond the most basic.

In the center of the room hang more white-painted boards. Each one displays photos of one particular branch, in no particular order, held on with thumbtacks and pushpins. Generally, the older photos are on top, but there are a lot of photos to fit in, a lot of people to identify across the years of formal portraits, Brownie snapshots, disc-camera pictures, digital images. You might see a young girl on a pony, then catch a glimpse of her at her wedding, see her surrounded by grandchildren, and then note another young woman who has similar prominent teeth. But wait—wouldn't that young woman be a generation further on? Must be the daughter.

You can study black and white posed tableaux of smoothly-groomed families with lots of children in sleek, polished rooms. But those are the older images. The newer ones are more likely to be hikes up mountains, ski excursions, prize fish, grinning grandkids. Comfortable clothes, rustic locales, downtime together. Two women outside a brick wall. Three kids on a grassy field. Names that recur. Faces that begin to look familiar.

"PLEASE do not make corrections directly on to the name tag or photo," a sign reads. "It looks messy! Use the clip-board located beside the 'Visitor's Sign In Table,' or complete the green card titled 'Missing Information.'" Do we need to add that this is all volunteer, a labor of love? The Visitor's Sign In Table is a folding one; if you need a chair, it will also be of the cheap folding variety. If there were a name or a motto on the front of this barn (an impossibility) it would be No Frills.

Actual books of genealogy have been published, with smooth paper and fine binding. But this is where the family seems to find its heart, in the snapshots sometimes identified with names of the cottages that are nearby; generations stilled, for a moment, in shorts or overalls, grinning from the bridge that you can just about see from the barn.

One of the folding tables displays Xeroxes of three obituaries from this year. The outlines of these people's lives —farming, teaching, business, military service, family—are not extraordinary, unless you count the mentions of this enclave where we find ourselves now. But these three lives are now finished. Their ending dates will be filled in on their little cards. There will be no new snapshots of them to squeeze into the spaces on the center boards.

When you are visiting, if you just need enough light to climb the stairs to the second floor, you can turn on the fluorescent lights from the switch at the door. Or, if you want to leave the lights on for a while so you can study the timeline or linger over the photos, perhaps searching out your own place in this neat arrangement, you can hit the buttons on the panel that give you ten, twenty, thirty, or even sixty minutes of light. If you do this, the sign says, "Do not attempt to shut the lights off by yourself. The lights will go off automatically." Eventually, all the lights in this room of the notable and the privileged, the ordinary ones and the lucky ones, will be dark.

Naming *the* Living *after the* Dead:
Oh Baby!

*W*ARNING: THIS CHAPTER CONTAINS MANY NAMES, some of which sound like some of the others. So just do your best, and know that a happy ending on a summer afternoon in Brooklyn is in store.

Jews typically name babies for family members, almost always of the same gender, who have recently died. It's a way to keep the memory of the person a little more "alive," as well as to give the newborn a model to live up to, a link to another soul. Primitive? You bet. Touching? Sometimes.

One lucky part of this practice is that the dead do not have feelings—not that they tell you about, anyway, and so they cannot be flattered or insulted. But the living do, and these slights and shout outs can have long lives of their own.

As if an impending birth were not cause enough for anxiety, consider the kinds of conversations, hints, nego-tiations, and asides that start popping up in Jewish homes as the due date draws near. Names of the recently departed are mentioned. Thoughts about various dead relatives surface. But there are hierarchies to consider. Was the dead person a family favorite? An estimable human being? Has somebody been named after that person already? Is this link being used to smooth over some family issue, or to forward some other agenda entirely?

Luckily there is some wiggle room. You can give the child whatever English name you like, but then use the dead person's Jewish name as the baby's Jewish name. So, for instance, little Samantha would most likely be Sarah for religious/ritual/life cycle occasions. This Jewish name is most often a Hebrew character from the Bible, but it can be Yiddish, which is a newer, more secular language. (Until the twentieth century, women did not necessarily have Hebrew names, because they were not eligible for . . . oh, let's not go there.)

Another option which is not gender-specific: you can go with a Jewish (generally Hebrew) name that starts with the same letter as the name, vernacular or Hebrew, of the person being remembered. You can even use the baby's middle name as the link.

As you can imagine, this can all get fairly attenuated. My sister's middle name is Frances, named for my father's grand-mother Frima, which is a Yiddish version of the Hebrew word for religious (the word is *frum*; the name became Fruma, with the pronunciation changing to Frima). Frima was the only one of my father's grandparents who made it to the New World, where he was born, and so the only one that he actually met. She was also the family member who died the closest to the birth of my sister. My parents did give my sister a Hebrew first name, Naomi, but that was another issue entirely. They just liked the name, and they liked the idea of having a Jewish first name. ("Show the bastards you're proud of being Jewish" was my devoutly secular father's credo.)

I have known my sister for a very long time, and never once has she or anyone around her ever said the word Frances. But when we were children, and my mother was feeling either loving or annoyed, she would call my sister by her Yiddish name, Nahumah Faigele, always followed by at least one exclamation point. *Faigele* means little bird, and is a nickname, sometimes used disparagingly, for gay men. So much for honoring Frima. The only story that has come down about her is that, when my father finally met her, he was already an adult, already a physician. She, however, treated him as a wayward little boy, jabbing him in the ribs.

It was not until I was grown up that I found out that the name of my aunt May, whom I saw every day, was actually Miriam, which was, after all, my name. In standard Jewish practice, it would have been out of the question to name me Miriam when we already had a living Miriam in the family; that would have been tempting the Angel of Death. But this situation seemed to pass muster because my aunt was never, ever called Miriam. Her mother, my grandmother, had named her after a beloved relative who had died young, in the Old Country. In practice, she could not bear to be reminded of the dead girl, so she called *her* little Miriam anything but: May, Maisie, Mamie. It was May that stuck. Just to make it more complicated, everything I have just described applies only to Askenazi Jews (Jews of Eastern European origin). Sephardic Jews (those whose ancestors lingered in Portugal or Spain) consider it an honor to name a baby after a living family member. What would happen if an Ashkenasi Jew married a Sephardic Jew? Don't ask.

But the naming impulse is a lovely one—to knit tighter the bonds of continuity, to give the newborn a gift. Sometimes this all works out, as in the case of my naming my daughter Mirka after my beloved grandmother, which we talked about earlier on. But it is easy to imagine how, as with any question involving family, heritage, loyalties, favoritism and superstition, the whole thing can become a minefield.

When my Mirka was grown up and slogging through her last month of pregnancy, she started getting worried about the name of her unborn child. She and her husband had a first name picked out that related nicely to my (dead) mother, and to her father-in-law's (dead) brother, both of whom luckily had names that began with the same letter. For the child's middle name (she knew it was going to be a girl), she wanted to do something nice for her late great-aunt Jennie, whom she loved dearly, and who had had no children of her own, and thus nobody to "claim" her name.

But then the worries began. First, there was Mirka's mother-in-law's mother, who was still alive, but not by much. If this frail woman were to die before the baby was born, there would be pressure, hard feelings, etc., etc.

Then there was Lester, who was Mirka's grandfather, my husband's father. He had died less than a year earlier. Nobody had been born in the family since, so no one had been named for him. Mirka did not have strong feelings about Lester. But his widow, Jeanette, Mirka's grandmother, did. (Sorry that Jeanette sounds so much like Jennie, Mirka's dead, and much

loved, great-aunt.) Jeanette let it be known that she was expecting something for Lester in the naming department.
People joked about Lesterina, but Jeanette did not seem to be
kidding.

Imagine Mirka, stomach huge, feet swollen, everything
swollen so much that she had to sleep with her arms above her
head so they wouldn't throb, spending her nights worrying.
Here was the solution she and her husband came up with:
When the baby was born, she was named Sadie Charna. Sadie
was for my mother Sally (Sarah) as well as for Stuart, the
brother of Mirka's father-in-law. I, in a gesture of extreme
magnanimity, decided not to make a fuss about the fact that
my (dead) father's name was also an S name (Saul) and why
weren't we including him in this package? OK, I could tell
myself; maybe we were. Didn't my parents have a set of
cocktail glasses with silver intertwined S&S?

By the way, just where did Charna come from? Charna
was the name (Yiddish) that great-aunt Jennie had been given
at birth by her immigrant Russian Jewish parents. But when
she started school in Canada, in the early years of the twentieth century, in a climate of assimilation, her kindergarten
teacher told her that Charna was flat-out impossible; she was
henceforth to be called Genevieve. Oy. Over the years, Genevieve morphed into Jennie. Charna became vestigial, but
Jennie maintained a soft spot for it. If you wanted to make her
very happy, you could give her, for a birthday present or
whatever, some article on which Charna was embroidered or
engraved.

When Mirka's baby was born, we told Jeanette (the baby's
great-grandmother—not to be confused with Jennie, who

would have been the baby's great-great-aunt) that the new baby's first name was Sadie, and that her Hebrew name was for Lester—Simcha Lila. (Simcha means gladness, or, by extension, a festive occasion.) Did little Sadie actually need yet another Jewish name? Actually no, given that Charna would already suffice. But we could do this for Jeanette because, really, what difference would any of it make?

Several days into little Sadie's life, Jeanette surprised us all by asking, "Did you know that my mother's name was Sadie?" Oh my God, we did not. This was extraordinary, but not surprising. My husband did not have any idea what his grandparents were named. (So much for all my careful explanations about tradition, continuity, etc., etc.) And, had we known, we maybe could have gotten away with just Sadie, and let Lester wait a little longer until the next addition to the family. But we were deep into it now.

In the meantime, Mirka was planning a naming ceremony for baby Sadie in New York, where they lived. My mother-in-law, Jeanette, who was in her nineties, was no longer capable of making the trip up from Florida, although we had offered to send somebody down to travel with her; or to pay for her aide to travel up with her. At the ceremony, I was to say a few words about my mother (Sally/Sarah) and my aunt (Jennie/Charna), and Mirka's father-in-law was to say a few words about his brother Stuart. We didn't need to exactly mention the Lester part because, although two of Lester's children (my husband and my sister-in-law) would be present, they were both cool with however this mass of taffy got pulled out.

Little did we know: the week before the naming ceremony, Jeanette, in the lonely comfort of her air-conditioned condo, began to feel very bad about missing this milestone event. She determined to surprise us by coming up to New York all by herself (something she had never ever done) and then staying with a cousin. Imagine our surprise when we found this out while we were scurrying around setting out the bagels and lox in the rented synagogue function room! Imagine us rushing over to my husband and telling him that Lester was now to be included in the "a few words about" lineup. Thank God my husband has always been able to think on his feet. To slice and dice the metaphor, Peter managed to conjure up a warm image of Lester where perhaps he had been most at home—behind the counter of the high end stationery store where he spent his days.

The naming event passed by in a blur. There were several kinds of smoked fish, and salads, and two kinds of *rugelach*, and lots of room for the little kids to run around. If anybody got confused about all the names, they were too busy greeting friends and relatives and chasing after their children to say so. And when I was correcting the proofs for this book and I checked in with my daughter about the spelling of Sadie's Hebrew names, she had no memory of whether she had settled on Lila or Lilah, given the fact that it might never be used at all.

If you have had trouble following this progression, don't worry. If you ever meet Sadie, she will be introduced with one name only. Should you ever pay a visit to her Hebrew school class (once she begins), or should you be present for her bat mitzvah or her wedding, or for when she has a role in a synagogue service, she will magically transform into Simcha Lila (or Lilah). And that, my friends, is quite enough of that.

What *to* Do *with* Those Ashes:
The Space *on* Susan's Mantle

BUT FIRST, A THEOLOGICAL DETOUR: FOR JEWS, cremation is never acceptable. Never. Because, although Jews do not focus on it, there does exist a concept of resurrection. And, if we all show up again, the sense is that it would be a very difficult thing to do if we could not find our bodies. It is one thing to return to dust in the earth, *au naturel*. It is quite another thing to purposely create that dust. And you can bet that, since the Nazis got so good at creating Jewish ashes, the cremation option has become even more unacceptable.

However. The one thing you can say about Jews is that they are never big on conformity. If there is some belief or practice that irks you personally, you always have an option: you can wring a different interpretation out of an ancient text, you can go find a rabbi, living or dead, whose opinion on the issue more closely matches your own, or you can decide that you don't like the whole debate in the first place, which obviously means that you can do whatever you want.

That last approach has been the one taken by my in-laws, Jeanette and Lester. If a thing is no bother, then that is the solution for them. If it is also cheap, then so much the better. For example, rather than buying a funeral plot and a stone, making sure the stone is correctly carved, paying every year for cemetery maintenance, then having to schlep out to Jersey or wherever the cemetery is located when you want to check in on your loved one, it makes so much more sense to just opt for cremation. Poof, and it's done. Oh, and they weren't sure they wanted funerals either. My in-laws started talking about these subjects after they retired to Florida, and could begin to imagine that they would not be returning North in any reasonable form.

For years, my husband argued with them: *You're being short-sighted, selfish and cheap,* he would say, trying to sound like he was being neutral. *Rituals are for the living. This is not about you.* But they were utterly indifferent to his point of view. After all, when they had left New York, where they had lived for the first six decades of their lives, they had gotten rid of their old furniture without any problem. Since then, they had been living the life they wanted in their retirement village. What on earth was to stop them from getting rid of their bodies the way they wanted? They were devoutly secular Jews who were thrilled by the freedom, the *no one is watching* aspect of America. (Their parents had all fled the disaster that was turn-of-the-last-century Eastern Europe.) Bottom line: My in-laws were going to do what they liked around death, especially if what they liked corresponded to doing little or nothing.

The first of their cohort to die was my mother-in-law's

brother Seymour, who had a heart attack on the toilet. He had married out of the faith and more or less out of the family; he would show up occasionally at family events, but he chose to keep his distance. He had made a life for himself centered on the military and on the Lions Club, neither of which struck a chord with his family of origin. His wife Tina was already dead, and they had no children.

After he died, we all schlepped to New Jersey, where Seymour was given a Lions funeral. (To show you I am not making this up, the motto of the Lions is, "Not above you, not below you, but with you.") There were a lot of flags and solemn faces, along with a lot of parading. We sat in the audience, and afterwards, Jeanette was given Seymour's ashes. She gave them to her daughter, Susan, who lives in Westchester and has a fireplace. Which means that, according to Jeanette's calculus, Susan has somewhere to keep ashes. On the mantelpiece, that is. In the cardboard box provided by the crematorium. Susan, who has a thing (positive) for pathetic animals, also inherited Pie, Seymour's half-Tibetan terrier, half who-knows-what, who had stayed in the house with the dead Seymour for a day until somebody found them, and who for the next several years dragged her arthritic rear end around Susan's house, piddling on the carpets and floors, never warming up to anyone in the family—feline, canine or human.

Next to go was Jeanette's sister Ann. Ann had two children, as well as a nice house with a garden. She did not have the same less-is-more attitude, but she was cremated as well. Her daughter talked a lot about sprinkling Ann's ashes around the lilac bush but, until she got around to it, Ann also spent several years in a box on Susan's mantle. Her daughter did eventually move Ann to the lilac bush. However, she has since sold that house. I wonder if the new owner knows why the lilac blooms so well. Eventually Pie, in a smaller box, joined Seymour on the mantle.

For Susan's fiftieth birthday, her parents, my in-laws, gave her a pair of urns which they insisted were not funerary urns. Funny, because that is exactly what they looked like. They were deep red enameled, with a tendril design. Susan did not like them, but she put them on the mantle, which was obviously where they belonged. She is a good sport, and a dutiful daughter. But she does have limited space on that shelf, so she kept needling her parents, who kept insisting, yes, they wanted to be cremated. And no, the idea of going into those urns had never occurred to them.

Fast-forward several years. My in-laws were in their nineties and, while their basic systems seemed to be doing more or less okay, some problems were becoming obvious. My father-in-law, Lester, had always had terrible eyesight, bad enough to keep him out of the Army in World War II. He had had two knees replaced when he was in his sixties and, although he had always been an active, athletic fellow, he was also very stubborn. He did not follow through on his physical therapy, so as he aged, his gait and his balance deteriorated. We hinted, encouraged, cajoled, hectored. Did he do his exercises? No.

He fell more and more often; one of his falls wrecked his "good" eye. Several of the falls resulted in broken bones and, when you are in your tenth decade, you don't heal very quickly. The normally mild-mannered man began to get grumpy. When he became incontinent, he totally lost patience with the whole thing. Life, that is. He didn't want to get out of bed. He didn't want to feed himself—not with his good hand; certainly not with the hand injured in his most recent fall. He only wanted to stay in bed, to the accompaniment of National Public Radio, and the regular beeping of his blind-person alarm watch, with its eerie electronic-man voice announcing the quarter hours.

My husband had always talked, in a bragging way, about how his paternal grandparents had died (different times, same m.o.): they just took to their beds, and that was the end of that. I pooh-poohed him. Until I watched their son Lester.

This did not happen the way you might imagine it, with some peaceful sense of having lived a good life, some touching Victorian-inflected scene of the children, grandchildren, maybe even great–grandchildren hovering. (Then again, my deathbed scene imaginings owe a lot to *Little Women*, in which the sainted Beth dies slowly and daintily, not wanting to be a burden, and her sister Jo writes a three-hanky poem.) Lester was in a bad mood and, the longer it went on, the worse his mood became. "Can't you just pay the doctor to come and give me a shot?" he barked. "Give him $5,000." He was not in any particular pain, except for the discomfort of impatience.

Meanwhile, Jeanette had been looking forward to celebrating their seventieth wedding anniversary, perhaps by taking the whole family on a cruise. (Forget the fact that several family members absolutely refused to set foot on the megaship that was Jeanette's dream.) She had been talking about it for decades, and this seemed to be the very last possibility. Lester, getting grumpier and grumpier, depending more and more on the two very decent and shamefully underpaid

Caribbean men who shared his round-the-clock care, was doing nothing to help her plan.

We did all show up for the seventieth anniversary. It was a takeout Italian meal in their Florida apartment, with Lester refusing to sit up, let alone get out of bed. When it got too depressing, we all crowded into the bedroom, stood around the bed and said things we remembered about Lester and Jeanette. Lester had zero interest in the proceedings.

He continued to get weaker and weaker. Just lying in bed will do that to you. After three or four months in bed, he died. Official cause of death? Failure to thrive.

There were a few days beforehand, when it was clear that Lester would not last long. At that point Jeanette relented, partly. She called the local rabbi, arranged to have a funeral. But there was no going back on the cremation. Susan, who was already in Florida, told her husband that, when he came down for the funeral, he should bring one of the urns to hold Lester's remains. When it was time for the funeral, at the Jewish funeral home, we had to smuggle it in, in a large paper bag. The funeral home people did not want their more observant clientele to know that ashes were being allowed through their door.

These days, both urns sit on the Formica sideboard in the Florida apartment. Jeanette says she talks to Lester in his urn. Her plan is that, when she dies, she will go into the second urn. She assumes that the family will keep the apartment in the retirement complex, and that the urns will stay on the sideboard.

In the meantime, Susan is thinking about selling her house, maybe moving to an apartment or a condo. One of the requirements of the place is that it not have a mantle.

THE WAY WE KEEP REMEMBERING:
THIS IS *a* PRAYER THAT YOU SAY
STANDING UP

ONE NIGHT RECENTLY, PETER AND I WENT TO FRIDAY night services at the Jewish community in the Vermont town where we have a ski condo. When we first started going there a decade a go, it was a pretty ad hoc group that met in a storefront. Now, even though the "spiritual leader" has gone to rabbinical school and been ordained, and they have built a lovely building, it is still a fairly low-key institution. Many of the members are second-home people like ourselves and, of the Jews who choose to live in this very non-Jewish neck of the woods, most are intermarried.

For us, it's been a base to touch, an easy way to socialize in a town where we spend time, but never dependably. We are often unsure of when we will come up for a weekend and, because we are likely to bring family or friends along, our local roots are pretty shallow. Still, this is where we "fit," a "third place" where we can feel at home.

Services that night had a focus—the music of Debbie Friedman, an enormously talented composer who had recently died. Using the traditional Jewish liturgy as her starting point, she wrote songs that are accessible and haunting. We sang several of them but, as it happened, it was a different part of the service that snuck up on me.

Jewish services have layers of standard components, built around set prayers recited in a set order. Depending on what denomination you are in, these recitations will vary in wording, length, and the proportion of Hebrew to the local secular language. But in general, if you attend a Sabbath service in any congregation in any part of the world, you can expect to recite, sing, or chant some part of this body of prayers. One that comes towards the end is the Mourner's Kaddish, the prayer associated with death. It is short—a total of seventy five words—and is a variant of a prayer that is recited in other parts of the service. But this iteration is reserved for mourners.

The strange thing about this prayer, which is always recited in the original Aramaic, the pre-Hebrew language spoken by ancient Jews, is that it does not mention death or anything related to it. Instead, it praises God and hopes for peace. It may be a prayer of propitiation (or desperation), with the implication being something like, *I am so weak and you are so strong; I hope you will take care of me at this time when I really need you.*

Another way to look at it is to think about death as the ultimate destabilizer of human experience. The goal of this prayer would then be to restore some of the balance to a world gone awry. The message of the prayer then would be, *Let's not talk about the bad thing that just happened. Let's instead reconfirm the power of God, and our hope for peace. Maybe God will be listening, and will restore to us something of that sense of peace that we are so missing right now.* Although the prayer is thousands of years old, its use by mourners may have started as a response to the slaughter of Jews during the Crusades.

Given such a long and complicated history, you can see how this prayer, like death itself, would be awash in unknowns. And, like so much of this ancient religion, the prayer has been the subject of many, many varying and conflicting interpretations. (Two Jews, three opinions, runs one of the most popular of Jewish jokes.)

The one thing that is indisputable is the prayer's incantatory power, which propels us along through a repetition of sounds that go beyond meaning. The writer Anita Diamant described it this way: "Syllable by syllable, shoulder-to-shoulder, Kaddish is a sigh that affirms the core beliefs and dreams of the Jewish people: God is beyond us. Understanding is beyond us. Holiness and beauty are all around us, but beyond us, too. We have work to do. There is hope. Peace is possible."

Reciting it can be a tall order when you are barely in a state to recite anything at all. When you are flat out with grief, furious at the world, the last thing you may want to do is to affirm the power of a deity who, at that moment, probably does not strike you as doing a particularly good job of running the universe. But sometimes it is helpful to have words, or sounds, that are expected to emerge from your mouth. Also, for a conflicted person like myself, the fact that these words are in a language you cannot understand can be a plus. (I am glad that I can understand the ending, though: *May he who makes peace in high places grant peace to us and to all Israel.*)

So this is how the process goes: If it is your time to say Kaddish (I will explain in a minute how you know when it's your time), you stand up, along with others scattered through-out the congregation who are also saying it, to intone the words that you may or may not comprehend. After every couple of sentences, the whole congregation joins you for a sentence or two. Then the Kaddish-sayers recite their part, then they are joined by the whole congregation again. It's not a call-and-response but more like a small group/big group orchestration. This, in itself, may be one of the strengths of the prayer. You are alone, but you are not alone. You are called on to speak, or at least mumble, but you are echoed, sup-ported. And what if you say nothing at all, because you are overwhelmed, despondent, furious, running your own little protest? The rabbi, or some other congregant, will speak the words, as if they never noticed your silence.

The very first time you recite Kaddish all the way through is likely to be the funeral of one of your parents. After that, depending on your brand of Judaism, you are meant to recite it anywhere from three times a day to once a week for a year and, after that, on the anniversary of the person's death. That date is referred to as a person's *yahrtzeit*, the Yiddish word whose literal meaning is year-time, or the time of the year when you remember that person. You are supposed to recite Kaddish for close family members who have died—a parent, sibling, or, God forbid, a child.

One of the objections that many people have to religion is

that it is hypocritical—people mouth pieties and then go out and do terrible things. I am not arguing against that concept. But Jews have a different tactic. Religion should put people's feet in the right place on the path. You cannot force them to walk further along that path, but you can show them where to begin. By regulating behavior, by expecting certain words, melodies, or actions at particular times, you help people to establish a "proper" way to live. If nobody tells you what is the right thing to do, then how will you know to do it?

If we were perfect, we would not need religion. So what Kaddish does is to give us a prompt for our emotions, a way to guide us into remembering and therefore honoring our loved ones. Feelings and thoughts bubble up. That is to be expected. But, with the ending of the prayer, we are guided into letting the dead recede into the background once again. The congregation turns the page and moves on—to the ending prayer, to the last song, to the refreshments and the socializing that always follow services. Enough with the sadness, this says, in effect. Let's get on with life.

Like many Jewish prayers, Kaddish must be recited in community. Jews need ten people in order to carry out certain parts of the service. (As mentioned before, the Orthodox count only men to make a *minyan*, or quorum.) This requirement means that there is a lot of running around looking for however many people are needed, a tense activity called "making a minyan" that is a staple of traditional Jewish life. A short story by the turn-of-the-twentieth-century author Sholem Aleichem called "The Tenth Man" riffs on this. Nine passengers on a train look for a tenth man so they can say Kaddish for the son of one of them, a young man who had been murdered by the police. They spot a man who is dressed as a non-Jew, but who they are all sure is just trying to pass. There are denials, negotiations, stories that may or may not be true; the standard range of devotion, disdain, innuendo, feint, that you are likely to find in a spectrum of Jews. But I am not about to give away the ending.

That kind of complexity shows some of the interplay of religious laws, customs, raw human need, the building and maintaining of community, all of which were operating that night in Vermont. We had gone to services for the easy sociability, and for the Debbie Friedman songs. But as I sat there knowing that Kaddish was coming up, the thought occurred to me that I would say Kaddish for my mother. We were a week early for her *yahrtseit*, but the odds were miniscule that I would find myself in a synagogue two weeks in a row. Normally I light a *yahrtseit* candle on the anniversary of the deaths of my parents and of my Grandma Millie. For a while I did it also for my aunt Jennie, who had no children, but I have sort of let that one slide. You can see my level of ritual observance: sorry, Jennie. And what about my other grandparents, or, for instance, Jennie's husband, or my other childless uncle and aunt? What are they, chopped liver?

Well, obviously I am a smorgasbord Jew, someone who picks and chooses only those parts of the religion she cares to observe.

If I were a "better" Jew, a more observant Jew, I would be tracking the dates of the deaths, all of the prescribed ones, according to the Hebrew calendar, a lunar calendar which differs from the Gregorian calendar we use in our "ordinary" lives. But I do more or less what I please, so I stick to the

Gregorian calendar. And, if you must know, I sort of skip saying the prayer and instead focus on lighting the *yahrtseit* candle which accompanies saying Kaddish at home. In my mind, it is lighting the candle that is important, but that is so totally backwards, and only reinforces my standing as a you-know-what kind of Jew. And here I have what I know is a lame excuse, but I offer it anyway: this is what my mother did. (Back to that later on.)

The other thing you need to know about reciting the Mourner's Kaddish is that you stand up to do it. When the rabbi reads off the names of the people reciting the prayer that week, sometimes you see somebody jump up; obviously they had forgotten all about it.

If it is your week, you sort of sneak a look around to see who else is standing. You form a little instant community, intimacy among strangers. You are on display. Sometimes that is good, and sometimes that is bad. Your pain (or lack of it) is public. Everybody knows your family status. Everyone can see if you are hurting. And then there are the standards: Do you look sufficiently mournful? Too mournful? Not mournful enough? Do you feel bereft, hopeful, angry, resentful, neutral, undone? And how much of that is bleeding out?

When you recite the prayer, sometimes you run on automatic, thinking something like, *it's been so long that they've been dead. I feel so little now. When it happened, I was overwhelmed with feeling. I thought it would never end. And look. It has.* And you stumble through the prayer or recite it with no thoughts at all. Sometimes, out of left field, the feelings flood back, and you can barely get through it, for the tears.

This time I thought about the distance between my mother and the North Woods setting in which I was saying the prayer. The idea of choosing to spend time in the cold, outdoors, in an athletic pursuit? That was so not my mother. She was born in Canada, spent much of her growing-up time in Buffalo, so she was no stranger to frigid weather, and she did enjoy physical activity to a certain extent, certain being heavily underlined. But to search it out? As she might have said, *nevvvvair!*

When, recently, my nephew was planning his wedding on the world-heritage-site-certified Mendocino coast, an outdoor playland for hikers, kayakers, etc., etc. (we discussed this wedding before; have you been paying attention?), my sister recalled that my mother had visited the place once years ago: "Very pretty," had been her verdict. "But there isn't anything to do."

So here I was, shivering and reciting Kaddish for a woman who not only avoided the cold, but who never went to synagogue. Still, she (religiously?) enacted many of the home-based Jewish rituals she had grown up with. Like lighting the *yahrtseit* candles.

Now that I think about it, I have no idea who she lit candles for, when I was a child and was being imprinted with *yahrtseit* lighting. I am pretty sure that my mother lit a candle for her mother-in-law. Although I didn't know her, my Grandma Lena did not have a good reputation; I know that she had been unwelcoming to my mother. How much more impressive, then, if my mother had done that (and wouldn't it have been my father's job, anyway, to remember his own mother?). Thinking it through now, I realize that my mother's own parents were alive throughout my childhood, and she had never known her grandparents, so the candle must have been for Lena. Way to go, Ma!

The occasion certainly impressed me. My mother bought the standard candle-in-a-glass, lit the candle at sunset, the correct "Jewish" time (the day begins at sunset), did not say the prayer (out loud anyway), then let the candle burn for its twenty-four-hour life, putting it in the sink overnight, just to be safe.

I feel like I have to say she was not religious, but here I may be wrong. There was a sense that what she was doing was important, and that sense of occasion, of gravity, that she brought to the endeavor has certainly stuck with me. Maybe that is a big part of what religion is.

When I was growing up, in poorer households the *yahrtseit* glasses were recycled to be used as drinking glasses— sort of a depressing thought, although I guess you could put a positive spin on it (death in the service of life, a glass of chocolate milk where despair once had been). And it's certainly eco-friendly. But my family was much too upscale for that. After the candle burned down, the glass got tossed. About a decade ago, the glasses shrank, from about an eight-ounce size to about four, from a pressed-glass design with arches to a plain cylinder that may be the same one that Catholics use. Did they figure out a way to get the candles to burn more efficiently? Let's hear it for progress!

That night, I asked Peter if he wanted to say Kaddish for his father, who, at that point, had been dead for less than a year, so a standup would have been appropriate. "No," he said, "he didn't want me to. But I'll say it for your mother." He has never, ever, volunteered to do this before. What moved him to do it? Was it a way of expressing whatever he could not express for his father? Or did he really have more feelings about my mother than about his own father? (A scary thought, but quite possibly true.) Let me just add that, whatever Peter's father might or might not have said about the subject, Peter could have recited Kaddish for him if he wanted to. As we know, it's all really for the living. And you can also make the argument that his father expressed his truly Jewish nature by being contrary. Perhaps the most widely-known Jewish joke involves a man, rescued from the desert island where he has been stranded for years. When his rescuers ask why he has built two synagogues he explains, "This is the one I go to for services, and that is the one I wouldn't be caught dead in!"

So Peter's substitution of my mother for his father, if that is what it was, would be highly irregular in traditional Judaism, but in the kind of congregation we were in that night, would have been par for the course. In addition to our private losses, we remembered Debbie Friedman, and the victims of a public shooting that had happened that week. Also, there are some people who always recite Kaddish on principle, for people killed in the Holocaust who have no one to recite it for them.

Peter and I mumbled our way through the prayer together. This night, after the prayer, the rabbi added the traditional response, saying, "May you and all the mourners of Israel be comforted." And yes, I found that touching. Even if it was rote, the rabbi has a manner that comes off as looking sincere.

After services, we all stood around for *Kiddush*, the snack of wine and challah named for the prayer over the wine—not to be confused with Kaddish, the prayer for the dead—and socialized. As we stood by the door, I saw two women hugging. The woman who had stood for Kaddish in front of me was saying that it had been two years now since her husband had died. Her eyes were wet. The woman who was hugging her was a widow whose husband, I happen to know, has been dead for quite some time. This was not a casual *feel better* hug. It was a hug that came from deep emotion for both of them.

Compared to these women, on this evening, my grief was pretty tame. My mother has been gone for almost twenty years. I was thinking about her, yes. But then I could go out into the night and I could think about what would be good to eat for supper.

How We Get Ready *to* Die:
Love Lies Bleeding

*M*Y FRIEND JOEANN HAS HER OBIT PHOTO ALL ready. She is standing in a garden, surrounded by eerie looking plants that feature large green leaves and even larger raspberry-colored fuzzy drooping pod-like things. They are so baroque that I wonder if it is some kind of joke.

If it is, the joke is a literary one. JoeAnn is a writer and a gentlewoman farmer. These are her favorite flowers, and they are called "love lies bleeding." *Amaranthus caudatus* has what are known as draping plumes; the deep red things make you think of tears. The chorus of the Elton John song of the same name ("Love Lies Bleeding," not "Amaranthus Caudatus") has a refrain that says, "And love lies bleeding in my hand. Oh it kills me to think of you with another man."

You may think that JoeAnn is being maudlin, or just controlling, but she has a reason. A year ago she was diagnosed with an early stage of the kind of cancer that killed Farah Fawcett, which makes it a celebrity cancer; slightly better than getting a proletarian cancer, but still, nothing good.

Last spring and summer, as she got driven to Boston for chemo, as she lay in the hospital getting the drugs dripped into her veins, as she got driven home for puking and sleeping and lying in bed feeling wan and spent, she had ample time to think about things like obit photos, and how she would like things to go if things didn't go so well.

But now it is a whole year later. She got through the chemo, has re-grown her hair and, most important, has muscled her way through some good test results. So when she went to visit her son, who was studying in Holland, and came upon a garden full of love lies bleeding she could, with some con-fidence as well as irony, pose for the photo. For her, Holland had not been about fields of tulips so much as about the triumph of these ridiculous-looking blooms. She had made the trip. She had walked and biked and ridden the canals. Maybe the amaranthus wouldn't be needed for a while.

She told me how, during the chemo time, she had made her husband promise that, if she died, he would never get married again. "I don't want some other woman in my house," she pronounced. I could see her point, but I couldn't resist asking, "What if the woman had her own house? What if they lived there?"

"Oh, he would never move," she said, case closed. Her conviction is well-founded. They have lived in their house together for thirty years and, before that, he lived in it with friends as a commune. The house used to belong to his grandmother. It is a sweetly charming antique. Although they have altered it over the years to suit their changing needs, it has—to state the obvious—a great deal of history.

I'm not sure how to say this, and as someone who is fairly

house-obsessed, it sort of surprises me, but I don't have that same sense of ownership—not just about my house, and not even about my husband. We have moved a couple of times, so I have learned that it is possible to drag yourself out of a place that you love, and that sets the stage for how you live, and settle yourself into someplace different, a place that, in time, you also come to love, and that also comes to define parts of you. (Before packing up the last two houses, I did walk around and photograph the rooms.)

I always assumed that, if I were to die (as if maybe I wouldn't! Maybe I should try that again: If I should die first), Peter would get married right off the bat. It's the kind of thing I tend to think about, in addition to having a back-up plan, or a day dream version of what would happen if . . . When I was younger, it was: if I dumped my boyfriend, or if things didn't work out, what other possibility was waiting in the wings? Later it was: who would I want to/who would I be able to marry if we got divorced? Now that, after forty or so years of marriage, that seems highly unlikely, I am more apt to think about: What would I do if Peter died, or what would he do if I did? (Of course this is all predicated on our dying before we get so old that we are totally out of it, although even that may not be the barrier it once was. You do hear these stories about people in nursing homes becoming attached to each other, even if they have a shaky understanding of "other," or "each.")

In recent years Peter has changed a little bit; he can tolerate solitude better, so it strikes me that he wouldn't necessarily get married right away, but I am guessing that he still would within two or three years. He still does not really like to be alone. And he is someone who appreciates/expects to live in an attractive, well-run home. But he is not the kind of person who could maintain that kind of operation himself, although he says he would just hire a housekeeper. If I tell you how closely our division of labor runs along the old sexist model you will be mortified for me. Or perhaps, if you are beyond all that, as I am, you will insert the all-purpose Yiddish afterthought *geyt gezut*: go in good health, meaning, eyebrows arched, what–*ever*.

And you know what they say about men remarrying right away: it shows that they had happy marriages. Well, did you ever think that for the wife it would just be sour grapes—the poor dead woman lying there rotting, and thinking, *yeah, well, rah rah; so it reflects well on me.*

Maybe it's because Peter and I both had "histories" before we got married. At the time, we were at the old end of the spectrum: I was twenty-six, he was twenty-eight—a joke now, I know. We both had had serious relationships; of course mine were more serious than his (weird form of bragging) but this may have been related to the fact that he was likely to move in with any girlfriend who had a reasonable apartment (see the housekeeping issue) whereas I was more into . . .what? By now it was so long ago, and, even if I could remember, I am not going to start dragging my old boyfriends into this discussion.

Still, we are talking about the next steps after a marriage that has been long and happy and productive, unquestionably good for both of us. Ages ago, we passed the point where we have been married longer than we have been not. And what, I don't even care? I can just say, *pfft* or *whatever? Bring on wife number two?*

I wouldn't want someone else to become Grandma to my grandchildren. (It's okay that they each have another REAL grandmother already.) No issue about my own children; they aren't exactly about to start calling somebody else Mommy or Mom. But here is the more likely outcome: even if the new wife is the most lovely, caring, fair-minded person in the world, she will have accumulated family/business/history/issues of her own, and so, not only will she spend less (far less!) time and energy and thought and caring on my offspring than I do but, because of how life works, the very presence of the new wife will make Peter less available to the kids and the grand-kids. So that's a big negative right there. The plus side is that, because she will provide company and caring for Peter, it will, to some extent, let his kids (my dear children) off the hook.

But do I care that somebody else will be settling into all the crevices of life with my husband, that the two of them will be making a life different from the one that we have shared all these years, that our very long timeline will end abruptly, and another line will start moving in a totally different direction? Maybe when I am lying on my deathbed this thought will reduce me to tears. Some other woman will be using my sock drawer! Maybe she won't even use it for socks! But now I am only thinking: just make sure my stuff gets stored where my grandchildren can get to it later on in case they want it. Rent a storage unit if necessary! There is way too much moisture in the shed and, over time, things left in it will rot.

Oy! So I am both materialistic and trivial. And I have learned nothing. After cleaning out the houses of various dead relatives and swearing that I would never leave all that stuff, stuff, stuff for others to deal with, you would think I would have ponied up and gone through all the things so the storage unit would be unnecessary. Well, just go back, Miriam, and read that last paragraph again. Get in there with your trash bag!

And what about my husband? Will he be sentimental and save my stuff? Will he always be thinking: *a year ago I was doing this with Miriam; Miriam always did this so much better than pathetic wife number two; oh, how I miss her* . . . He is a gruff and unsentimental sort, and so I think no, not really. But in actuality, when I am sick he gets very upset. (Is that because he is afraid I am about to die, or just because I am for the duration incompetent? I have already told you about the issues around household management.) Weird, how I cannot conjure up what would seem to be the appropriate level of emotion around this. Time to change the subject.

JoeAnn planned out her funeral, thought about who she wanted as speakers, what music she wanted played. Maybe if I were lying in the heat in a chemo haze, I would be doing the same thing.

But here is how I came to understand how little of life beyond the grave you can imagine, let alone control. When I brought up the subject of remarriage recently with Peter, his response brought me up short. "Why would I have to get married?" he said. He and the new girlfriend could just live together. Geez, I just about slapped my forehead. I had been projecting my own thoughts, not channeling Peter, who would, as usual, be five steps ahead, playing the angles. He hadn't wanted to get married the first time around. Why should he have a different opinion all these many years later? (Goodbye to my sock drawer! Maybe it will retain a whiff of my lavender sachet for years. Maybe that will be my meager revenge.)

Or maybe I should decide that this is all a compliment to me; that Peter's opposition to marrying again means that I would always be the real wife, the one true love; that the successor would just be a "companion" or, as they sometimes say in obituaries, "dear friend." People always say that, if you have children together, you are never really "not married." But how about if one of you is dead?

Oh, my poor successor. She will have the demanding and entitled and grieving biological family to deal with. (At least I assume they will be bereft. I can only pray that my loved ones will be inconsolable, forlorn, hopefully for years.)

Let's hope that the new non-wife has her own house, her own life, her own relatively thick skin. I would hate to be the person stepping into my (well-worn and idiosyncratic) collection of shoes.

STAGING *a* FUNERAL:
OPEN CASKET

*Y*OU MAY FIND IT INTENSE TO HAVE AN OPEN CASKET at a wake or a funeral. But consider, for a moment, just how intense it would be to dig up your loved one a year later on so you can open the coffin and stare death in the face.

Ralph Waldo Emerson did just this in 1832. A seeker after authentic experience (no kidding!), he went on to become one of our great thinkers. He has been called everything from America's first existentialist to the "Hindoo Yankee." At the time he pried back the coffin cover, though, he was a grieving and not-very-successful young Unitarian minister.

Emerson's much-loved wife, Ellen, had died of tuberculosis when she was just shy of her twentieth birthday, and Emerson was bereft. He continued to write to her in his journal as if she were alive. Every day, he would walk from Boston to Roxbury, an invigorating trip, to visit her grave. The day of the opening was actually a year and two months into his mourning but, frustratingly, in his journal he gave us (you should excuse the expression) only a bare bones report: "I visited Ellen's grave and opened the coffin." No *how did she look,* let alone *smell; no how did it feel, what did the neighbors think, where did I ever come up with such a crazy idea.* On the day after he dug her up, and for months thereafter, he continued his daily walks to Roxbury.

But seeing the real decay, the ineluctable deadness of his beloved, seems to have helped him through his crisis. Two months after he opened the grave he wrote, "Let us address our astonishment, before we are swallowed up in the yeast of the Abyss." So, evidently, reality won out; life triumphed over, or at least displaced, death. Emerson resigned his pulpit, auctioned off his furnishings and took a ship bound for Europe, where he traveled for a year, meeting several of the great writers and intellectuals of the day—John Stuart Mill, William Wordsworth, Samuel Taylor Coleridge, Thomas Carlyle. He also sued his in-laws to get his share of his dead wife's money.

In time, Emerson came home and remarried. His new wife, Lydia, whom he renamed Lydian, a word with more intellectual heft, knew that she could never compete with the beautiful dear dead Ellen. It was she who recommended that, when they had a baby girl, they give her Ellen's name. Or maybe she was thinking, *get Ralph to have a different association with that name. Get his mind off of her.* They also had a son, Waldo, and two other children. When Waldo was five, he died of scarlet fever. Fifteen years after Waldo's death, twenty-five years after the death of the first Ellen, when Emerson was relocating the grave of little Waldo, he decided to open that coffin as well. Again, frustratingly, no comment.

These acts may not have struck contemporaries as so bizarre as they strike us now. Emerson's biographers, Robert

D. Richardson and Barry Moser, tell us that another Unitarian minister of the period opened the coffin of the woman he had loved. And Rufus Griswold—an anthologist and literary type whom we know about, if we know about him at all, because he was Edgar Allan Poe's literary executor as well as his nemesis (a strange story worthy of Poe himself) —was so distraught over the death of his wife in 1842 that he kept her body next to him for a thirty-hour train trip, kissing her while their two young children wept beside him. Forty days after her death he opened her vault, cut a lock of her hair, and kissed her some more. He stayed with her overnight, until a friend came and dragged him away.

These bizarre acts are not limited to the nineteenth century. In 1930, Georg Karl Tanzler, a German-born physician working in Key West under the name of Carl von Cosler, fell in love with one of his patients, Maria Elena Milagro "Helen" de Hoyos, a young Cuban-American beauty. When she died of tuberculosis the following year, he visited her body in her family's mausoleum every night. One night, two years later, he put her body in a toy wagon and wheeled it to his house. I will skip over the details about holding the bones together with coat hangers, replacing the skin with silk cloth soaked in wax and plaster of Paris. It wasn't until 1940 that the authorities got wind of what was going on, showed up at his house and took the body. It was displayed at a local funeral home and viewed by close to seven thousand people. In 2005, when HBO covered this story, they included allegations of necrophilia, but had no hard evidence.

Weird stories, of course. But who among us does not understand the impulse behind these events? Let's also admit that, in the cold light of day, our contemporary practices can seem strange as well. We take the opposite tack—outsourcing death and burial, averting our gaze from the plain fact of decay.

I have no memory of either looking or not looking at the bodies of my dead grandparents, when I was a child and teenager, so I was either traumatized or nonplussed. My father's death when I was forty did not come as a surprise. He had been suffering from congestive heart failure for years, had had a couple of heart attacks. When a particularly bad one left him comatose in the I.C.U., I drove down from Boston to New York and went with my mother to the hospital, then to a deli for supper (most likely brisket sandwiches with coleslaw on the sandwich, a favorite of both of ours), then went home with her where, exhausted, we soon fell asleep. She answered the phone when it rang at five a.m. The message was not a surprise, but that didn't give the experience any more reality, as we drove back to the hospital in the pitch dark.

He was just where we had left him the night before, in the bed next to the window. My mother, whose feats of emotional control were legendary, walked over to him and ran her hand along the length of his arm.

"He's still warm," she said in an oddly quiet voice. "Come here and feel." She was the nurse. I was the grown up version of the little girl who had done her best to avoid the medical emergencies that showed up in my father's office. (We lived upstairs.) *This is good for you,* I lectured myself. *Take his hand.*

In some ways, he was the same as always—his large bones, his solid presence. But something was unrecognizable.

"Glasses," my mother said. "Where are his glasses?" Of course I had seen him barefaced occasionally, when he had been woken up in the middle of the night to go see a patient, but when my mother found his glasses and gently put them on him, he looked more like himself. Except that he was un-moving, glassy, waxy, a little too pink. (He had had a high fever. When we had left him he had been quite pink and quite warm.)

I was almost as shaken by my mother's tenderness toward him (they had a physical ease with each other, but also a wary formality, even after more than four decades of marriage) as by the fact of his death.

In our family, during funeral home visiting hours, we have gone for the open casket, making sure that it is in a corner so people don't have to see the dead body if they don't want to, and then closing the casket before the funeral.

I find that I kind of get used to having that box in the corner, or having that box in the corner that I try to ignore. Still, I push myself to spend some time with the body. *It's what you're sup-posed to do*, I tell myself, although I answer back, *What makes you so sure? Why can't I just skip this part? And besides, is this how I want to remember them? Or how I want to remember feeling?* I try to talk to the dead person in my head, making sure to say good-bye, as my old therapist would have encouraged, even though my husband makes fun of that dutiful part of my makeup, and even though I sometimes wonder if we are slip-ping into the world of magical thinking here: *If I say the right thing, I will be able to grieve "properly." If not, I will forever wriggle around in some Purgatory of the Unexpressed.* Still, I am not taking any chances. If I think there is something I should be saying to the person, I will try to get myself to say it. Luckily, the person is dead, and anyway, I am not talking out loud.

But sometimes, the dead belong not to us, but to the public. Sometimes, coffins are opened, even after burial, for purposes of identification. Abraham Lincoln's casket was opened a remarkable seven times because, despite being topped with a layer of cement, rumors persisted about the wrong body being placed in his tomb, or the right body being stolen. The last opening was in 1901, thirty-six years after his death. And, for another sixty years, arguments continued over who was the last person alive who had seen Lincoln's body.

For those viewers, though, it had only been about witnessing. For Emerson, and for Griswold, and for who knows how many others, it had been about giving up hope, about facing unfaceable facts. Emerson once wrote about lovers: "*When alone, they solace themselves with the remembered image of the other.*" If the "other" was only rot and decay, that would surely change the solace equation.

We can all identify with Emerson's morbid curiosity, with his need to convince himself that his loved one was, in fact, no more. Even in the same way that rumors persisted about Lincoln's body going missing, we find it difficult to give up the hope that our dead may not actually be gone. No matter how rational and sane we are, we still half expect to catch a glimpse of them on the street; sometimes for half a second we are convinced that we do.

Mold and compacting and disintegration are only physical facts. The real "facts" are emotional. And we will do anything in our power to avoid them. Emerson wrote, about grief: "*Sorrow makes us all children again—destroys all differences of intellect.*" On this subject, the brilliant sage said, "*The wisest knows nothing.*"

MOURNING HOW-TO:

FOR BRILLIANT PEOPLE WHO, THROUGH NO FAULT *of* THEIR OWN, FIND THEMSELVES HACKING OUT THEIR OWN PATH THROUGH *the* DENSE WOODS

THIS BOOK HAS FEATURED A LOT OF MEANDERING. But wherever I've gone, I've come back to a well-established starting place. My family, my ethnic group, my religion, have very clearly defined rituals, practices, habits, and beliefs around death and mourning. But what if you find yourself far from a religious or ethnic tradition, alienated from standard ritual, not part of a close-knit traditional community?

Then you can just go hog wild. Even as wedding couples of all faiths or no faiths, these days, are likely to find themselves lifted up above the crowd in chairs, screaming with delight and nerves, mourners, along with their friends and families, may find the concepts of *shiva*, or home altars, or wakes—or some version of the above—helpful in, and this may sound gross, *getting the most* out of a difficult time.

You will have lots of options: quick burial, like the Jews. Ritualized washing of the body, like the Muslims. The idea of a four-day period between dying and rebirth, as in some parts of Buddhism. Or how about looking up the Colorado organization that helps people who live in the area arrange outdoor cremations? As for long-term remembrance, some cultures mark one particular day to honor all their dead, while in others, it's the anniversary of the person's birth or death that become the prompts for recollection.

But why stop there? Check out the American company that will produce what it calls a diamond from the ashes or hair of your beloved. "We also have a full line of cremation jewelry, rings, and pendants," they inform us. Or you could just get a t-shirt commemorating the company's tenth year in business. Hey, it's a smorgasbord world. If you don't live in a close community, you can do whatever you like.

When Coco Chanel's married lover died in a car crash at the age of thirty-eight, she re-made her bedroom. She had the furniture covered in black. She had black curtains made for the windows. She put black sheets on the bed. But when she entered the room of sadness, she realized that she could never sleep there, so she had her butler make up a bed for her in another, more forgiving room.

After my father died, we spent a few days at my mother's, where she sat *shiva*—which, in our attenuated Jewish practice, meant that she stayed close to home—and people came by, bearing deli platters and cake. When we came back to our home from my mother's house, I really didn't feel like continuing the *shiva*, which traditionally lasts for a week. The truth was, I really didn't feel like doing anything. Except maybe climbing into bed. I told myself that maybe I was sick, so that is why I wanted to get into my nice warm bed and pull the comforter up around me in the middle of the afternoon. Eventually, I told myself that maybe there was no difference between having a flu and feeling wrung out about the death. So I got into bed after lunch, and I stayed there until the kids came home from school.

So the first thing you might want to do is to be kind to yourself. Help yourself over the immediate hump. And then help yourself over the next one. And the next one after that. Just don't look for easy solutions. I had a very well-bred aunt who said, "Whenever you are thinking of saying bullshit, just say fantastic." So:

The five stages of grief are fantastic.

The arbitrary time markers around any sort of resolution of feelings are fantastic.

The idea that you will move forward in a straight line toward "resolution" is fantastic.

And here I mean that fantastic connotes not only bullshit, but also being rooted in fantasy. We would so much prefer it if grief could move tidily along, like the big hand on the cuckoo clock, ticking off the minutes until, *Poom!* The clock makes it up to the twelve, the birdhouse door springs open, out pops the cuckoo and announces that it is all done.

Real grief, however, has its own inscrutable timeline. Just when you think you are getting some firm footing, another wave of grief comes out of the ocean of misery and slaps you down. Other times, when you think you should be barely able to stand, you feel embarrassingly jaunty and ready to take on the world.

I have already mentioned my friend who said that, after her husband died, she found the second year the hardest. Another friend, Sally, several years into widowhood, said, "Each season without him, I say, I can't see how I can go through another season without him." In the early days of grieving, this normally upbeat person felt out of sync with the rest of the world. Even if a dear friend would invite her for lunch, she said, "I just didn't want to go for a jolly meal."

But here is another way of looking at it. Because the only thing you can count on is that things won't go the way you expect them to, the door is wide open for creativity, for following your heart. Right after Sally's husband died, she couldn't sit still, couldn't get anything done. Her friend offered to come to the house and just sit there for a while, doing some of her own work.

Sally was highly dubious. But in fact, just having someone in the house let her calm down enough to focus and do some of the things she needed to tend to. Instead of her friend making the vague *call me if you need anything* offer, Sally said, "She knew enough to offer it. I didn't even know I needed it."

Still, it's a great help to be able to fall back on ritual, your own or somebody else's. Feel free to repurpose or re-appropriate any tradition that appeals. This may also be a time when you find yourself drawn to the religion or tradition you thought you had been happy enough to discard. And that's fine too. But look for more innovation than tradition in the years ahead.

We Americans are big on reinvention. As the "Me" generation of baby boomers heads out into the great beyond, we can expect quite a range of behaviors, from the ultra-traditional to the do-it-yourself. Hey, aren't we the people who invented the one-day clergy license, the online ministry certification? Just as we are making our wedding ceremonies more individual, more about *us*, we are doing the same thing as we approach our ends.

Here is the most recent death notice that popped up in my in box: . . . "Survived by her three sons . . . and her two grandsons . . . Memorial/Party service to be held at two p.m. Sunday . . . (colorful and comfortable attire requested, dogs on leash and Frisbees welcome)."

If this is what appeals to you, then feel free. But I would like to get you to go a little bit deeper. I understand the impulse of the memorial/party. I really do. I am betting that, even if my Frisbee-loving friend did not tell her sons that this is what she wanted, she gave them enough cues to allow them to set up this kind of event. After all, if we are happy, decent people, why would we want to make our dear ones miserable? Isn't it more satisfying to think of ourselves as being the impulse for, the subject of, a day in the park with Frisbees and dogs (on leashes)?

Well, no. Because death is not fun. And, at the risk of sounding like a certain bearded Austrian fixated on conversion hysteria, if we don't deal with our sadness in one place, we shouldn't be surprised to see it pop out in another. Those sons and grandsons with their Frisbees and their dogs—isn't it weird to expect them to be making of this mega-transition a day in the park?

We Americans are great at doing confident and happy. Our civic religion involves finding our bliss, choosing something that makes us personally fulfilled, and then going after it. What we aren't so great about doing is appropriate sadness or grief. And even though we are one of the most "religious" countries around, we are not so big on tradition, community, or spirituality. I think we are getting better about respecting multiculturalism, but if the benefit of immigration and restless mobility is getting rid of our old baggage, the price is losing where we have come from.

As you have undoubtedly noticed, I appreciate the healing powers of ritual. Because, guess what: we are not the first people to die. And because, as long as people have been dying, other people have been figuring out ways to live with this. Death is just too hard a business to have to figure out the whole thing from scratch, inventing practices and strategies at a time when our intellectual and creative powers might not be at their best.

One of the reasons I wrote this book was to help people think about these things, talk about them, make plans, preferably well before the crisis. The deathless word coined by the funeral industry is *pre-planning*. I don't mean that you have to sign on the dotted line, but it does help to give some thought to where you stand, where you would like to lie, and then let your family know what you are thinking.

For some families, these will be tough conversations. But they are not going to get any easier if they are taking place, forgive the pun, on deadline. I recommend starting off with a little black humor, and just jumping right in. Perhaps we can invent a funeral game: *I'm thinking of a part of a funeral that begins with . . . say . . . S.* The correct answer there would be slideshow; and then you can decide if having a slideshow would be gross or gorgeous, and you can describe what would sway your opinion either way. Another game would be *Would you believe . . .* in which people take turns describing the strangest funeral they have attended or heard about. The euphemism game is endlessly funny: from dearly beloved to free worm food; from the garden of the sleepers to south of the frost line. Once you have begun this conversation, I hope you will keep it up. Because life will continue to present us with new examples all the time.

For a hint as to one direction these talks might take, listen to this "funeral concierge" quoted recently in *The New York Times*: "The body's a downer, especially for boomers. If the body doesn't have to be there, it frees us up to do what we want. They may want to have it in a country club or bar or their favorite restaurant. That's where consumers want to go." Or how about the academic paper that says, "While the funeral industry can be characterized as selling both a product (casket, headstone, etc.) and an experience (i.e., the funeral service), historically it has been the product side (especially caskets) that has provided firms with their primary revenues." But, because of the increasing popularity of cremations, the product side of the business has been declining. So the experience side will become the new business model. Since we embrace themed institutions like "Hard Rock Café or Planet Hollywood, Disney cruises, Las Vegas hotels, Niketown, etc.," we are advised to look for more camping funerals, motorcycle funerals and knitting funerals in the coming years.

Above all, look for more celebrations of life, more memorial services, more funerals. Because one of the few things we can say with certainty is that death never gets old.

WHERE I'M GOING:
CLEARING *in the* WOODS

*I*F YOU ARE LOOKING FOR THE JEWISH CEMETERY IN Gloucester, it is best to drive very, very slowly. There is a sign, but it is so small that you can read it only if your car is already stopped and you are looking straight at it. It is pretty much hidden behind a tree, and the paint is half gone.

The highway is actually quite nearby but, by the time you have parked your car and walked up the path to this flat clearing at the bottom of a bowl of wooded hills, you hear only the wind, the trees, and your own heart. Unless you are very familiar with this territory, having hiked it or flown very low in a small plane, you would not imagine that this sea-facing peninsula contains such large swaths of forest.

When I arrive for a cemetery visit, my first nod is typically to a grave in the front row. Daniel was in my son Eli's Hebrew school class. His mother was, and is, my friend. He was adopted. He was difficult. In time, he had a diagnosis—Tourette's Syndrome. Impulse control problems. Dead of an overdose at thirty-one. *No fear*, his mother inscribed under his dates.

But most of the graves in the front section are old. These dead have been here half a century or more. Many of the family names are familiar from my days as synagogue president; some of the families have relatives whom I know.

This is so different from the large-scale New Jersey Memorial Park of my youth. But this type of small woodland clearing is pretty standard practice in New England, where I have lived all of my adult life. Both Jews and Christians make these small plots, setting out graves in rows. For Jews, if you want to orient them anywhere, the most common direction is facing toward Jerusalem. Sometimes, I have learned, in Christian colonial cemeteries, the congregation would be buried in a semicircle facing the minister, so that, when the day of judgment came, everyone would be ready to take their cues from him.

One creative exception is the Sedgwick Pie, in Stockbridge, Massachusetts. The Sedgwicks are an old New England family with many civic-minded high achievers. Beginning in the eighteenth century, the Sedgwicks, along with their in-laws, servants and pets, were buried in concentric circles with their feet toward the center, where their founder was buried. The idea was that, when the Resurrection came, they would only have to face other Sedgwicks. (Irresistible side note: Civil War general John Sedgwick is known mostly for his last words at the Battle of Spotsylvania Court House. When Confederate sharpshooters closed in, and his men started taking cover, he strode through the battlefield saying, "What? Men dodging this way for single bullets? What will you do when they open fire along the whole line? I am ashamed of you.

They couldn't hit an elephant at this distance." When this tale is told, his words are sometimes quoted as " . . . at this dis—" because he was, of course, picked off).

On this fall visit to our little cemetery, I catch sight of a new mound of earth. It belongs to the father of my friend Mitch, whose death started this whole project for me. He was old and frail when Mitch died; no one was surprised that he didn't last long. On the day that Bernie was born, a different Bernard in the congregation died; they also had the same last name, although they were not related. In some sense, though, we are all related. That older Bernard's grave is here too.

I am not surprised that Bernie, Mitch's father, has a prime location, just next to the asphalt path that runs the length of the place. He was a sociable man who lived here for most of his life. When I arrived, thirty years ago, all I heard about was Sylvia, his wife, then recently dead. Her side of the double stone is engraved. His side of the stone, empty now, will be filled in soon.

When I come here, I keep track of my friend Wendy out of the corner of my eye, as if she were about to spring up and greet me effusively, ready with some athletic or artistic or social project, or offering up some cockamamie idea. She and her husband have two stones that stand on the same base. The two of them are set off, with no other stones immediately around them. Ironic. Really ironic. Lousy marriage, and now the two of them are two upright stone pillars, forever stuck to a single base. I keep track of where Wendy is, but I am not ready to go see her yet.

It is fall, and the day has been off-and-on rain. It's between Rosh Hashanah and Yom Kippur, the Days of Awe, the time when we are supposed to take stock of our lives, when we rehearse our own deaths, when we come to visit our dead. My family is elsewhere, but it would not be lying to say that these are my dead.

I notice Marty and Alice, parents of my friend Steve. Alice: 2009. *She added beauty to the world.* Marty: 2003. *Only to do justly, to love mercy. And to walk humbly with your God.* For a time before Marty got sick, before Alice went gaga, we had several conversations with them about buying their house, but Alice had no interest in moving.

I visit our bench. Some years ago I got it into my head that this was what the place needed. My husband Peter and I bought it and had it set down off on the left side, sheltered by a slight hill. I knew how great it was to have some place to sit, because of our bench in New Jersey. This one is rough-hewn granite, more generously sized than the New Jersey one. Whoops, and now it is growing lichen. I will have to find out what to do, come back with pails of water, brushes, cleaning agents. This is a do-it-yourself cemetery. Except for the actual digging of the graves, we do everything here. Sometimes it feels good to do the work; the weeding, the pruning, the filling in of the grave. Today I don't even want to think about it.

Once I have reassured myself that I will only stay for a minute, won't make myself stay, I am ready to visit Wendy. And all the time I am telling myself: *This is good. I don't feel so terribly sad. I am not overcome with the sound of her voice, with images of her.* She is farther away in time, dead for more than a decade now, and I am only sad, not miserable. I am no longer worrying about who should be doing what, who should be taking care of the kids. Her kids are grown. Her absence has become the norm.

The style of Wendy's stone is slightly ornate, and feels kind of off-the-shelf. But then Wendy and her husband were never good about planning. I am trying to remember if they did the base and stone configuration when Wendy died. Highly unlikely. Who would have expected her husband to die three years later? I am glad to see that more people have left the little *we were here* stones on Wendy's side. But she was always more popular, even if he is the one who made a mark on the world.

When we were still in our thirties, Wendy, Sandie, Andrea and I started a little publishing venture. We used to joke about how we would grow old together, scooting in our wheelchairs in the old age home. When we shifted the venue of our jokes to the cemetery, we never for a moment thought that one of us would be moving here so soon.

At some point, I will move here as well. Although in one sense it is hard to imagine, in another sense I can absolutely picture it. I have been to many burials here. I know very well how they go, with the mourners standing stoop-shouldered, in sweltering heat or freezing cold. It is traditional to throw in a symbolic shovel full of dirt; hearing that noise really brings it all home, but since we fill in the entire grave ourselves here, that adds another level of reality.

Peter and I have plots near the bench. I can imagine my kids coming to visit, thinking the kind of blank thoughts I have when I visit my own dead parents, when I let my feelings burble up. Maybe they will have as hard a time leaving as I do. But I will not notice. I tell myself that, but what is more difficult to imagine then not being able to imagine?

In the meantime, out front, Daniel is keeping watch. That is what his mother says anyway. He was incredibly strong; he liked to show off how he could lift a car. Not a lot of judgment, but more than his share of brawn. In the time since Daniel has been in the cemetery, there have not been any incidents. (This is, after all, a Jewish cemetery in the middle of the woods. Things can happen, and, every once in a while, they do.) In the years that Daniel was alive, things did not go easily for him. But he is in a quiet place now, encircled by people who have (had?) his interests at heart.

Maybe we are a bit like the Sedgwicks—buried here with our own, taking our personal and group solace in this quiet, sheltered spot.

Regrets:

Tood's Birthday

*E*VEN AT THE TIME, I SOMETIMES THOUGHT IT WAS A little bit strange that Mildred was one of my very best friends. She was a good twenty years older than I; she had had polio as a young woman and was in a wheelchair; her children were just a few years younger than I was; she was definitely more *lah-di-dah*, although in a Cambridge sort of way (I'll get back to that later if you want clarification).

Now I think—you can go on from now until Doomsday about how people are different (her hair was super-curly, while mine is as straight as if I were Chinese or Dutch; she grew up in Kalamazoo; she was small and kept herself thin, since it was often necessary for her husband to carry her). The real fact, the important fact, the only fact, is this: we connected, and stayed connected, without interruption, for twenty years. We saw each other often. We each occupied that privileged place in the other's life in the circle that is just beyond immediate family. There was a period when we spoke to or saw each other pretty much every day.

I don't think I'm giving anything away here if I say that

the reason we are no longer friends is that Mildred ended the friendship by dying. Not that it was her choice; not that she didn't know her risk factors and do her best to best them. She did, but in the end, she didn't. She probably had the bad breast cancer gene. She certainly had the bad breast cancer family history. So she upped her mammograms and her doctor visits. Her diet was aggressively healthy even without the cancer risk. But it was the breast cancer that killed her, and relatively quickly, at age sixty-two.

I met Mildred when I was just out of college, an aspiring filmmaker. I was the assistant to a woman who was using Mildred's family to shoot a contemporary version of a Thomas Mann short story called "Disorder and Early Sorrow." It was about a professor's family, and yes, Mildred's husband was a popular and attractive Harvard professor. Jim, their almost-adult kids, their kids' friends, and their house all played starring roles, but the filmmaker did not want Mildred in it because of the wheelchair—it complicated the story.

This struck me as being both understandable and heartless, but Mildred handled it well. By that time she had spent twenty years in the chair; she knew very well how to live her life sitting down (this was before laws about handicapped accessibility, before ramps, before accessible bathrooms) but, she said, when she dreamed, she was still walking and dancing. (Before marriage and children, she had been a dancer, had trained with Martha Graham.) Every morning when she woke up, she was slightly surprised and disappointed when her eyes fell on the chair.

The family adopted me at once, and I fell into an easy relationship with them, although they were a good couple of notches up from my Bronx family in terms of money, class, and worldliness. The house was full of art, music, and people across a very broad age range who were Doing Interesting Things. There was a casual approach to a lot of high-end stuff, and an assumption that everyone was more or less connected. It was flattering, fun and energizing to be part of this crowd.

A couple of years later, when Peter, at that point my New York boyfriend, applied for a job in Cambridge, we didn't know it, but one of the people on the board of the hiring organization was Mildred's husband. After the interview, Jim took Peter home for a drink, where Mildred asked him why he wanted to move to Boston. His fiancée lived there, he explained. Mildred, of course, needed to know all about this fiancée. When he told her, she laughed her big laugh and said, "That's no fiancée, that's our Miriam!"—a phrase we treasured for years.

Tood was Jim's special name for Mildred. Her name for him was Bim. They told us how, for some people, polio destroyed the marriage. For others, it made the marriage stronger. They thought of it as "our polio."

Because they loved to cultivate interesting young people, Peter and I were not their only young friends. But we stuck. We spent time together at their aggressively unimproved Vermont farmhouse. When Jim had a year's residency at the American Academy in Rome, we visited them for a week, and I showed my films there. It was terrifying to push Mildred's wheelchair through the wild Roman traffic; apart from the fawning nuns, nobody gave her an inch. I, on the other hand, was pregnant, and got a lot of attention (although no milk to drink, only wine).

Back in Cambridge, I often visited Mildred with my kids, who were wary of Tosh, their elderly and crabby Dalmatian, but they loved to ride on Mildred's lap in the wheelchair. She had given birth to her third child post-polio. Even as a tall adult, Sarah, that child, enjoyed climbing onto her mother's lap. Every day Mildred had to "stand up" for an hour, which meant supporting herself on her crutches in the backyard. This was the time she liked to have someone come over and talk. Mildred began making arty films, so lots of our talk revolved around that.

She was a serious do-gooder, health faddist, knee-jerk liberal. She gave us a voting booth crib sheet that made it easy to navigate the mind-spinning world of Cambridge politics. She called the black cleaning lady Mrs. Mack, while Mrs. Mack called her Mildred. The household stopped for the after-lunch hour when Mrs. Mack watched her soap opera.

Mildred was also totally engaged in the lives of her family, friends, and neighbors. When Peter and I came to visit them in Rome, she was so excited that the day before we arrived, she got a migraine.

In the mid '80s, we moved to a small town an hour away, but our renovation included making our kitchen and downstairs bathroom accessible, thinking of Mildred. Soon after, she got the bad diagnosis.

There is only one thing in my life that I really regret: When Mildred was well into the cancer, it was her birthday. She only wanted a couple of people beyond the immediate family. I was one. But that weekend we were due in New York for my father-in-law's seventy-fifth birthday, a big event. I should have stayed behind to be with Mildred. (And yes,

Mildred lived for a couple more months, and yes, I did see her a couple more times. But clearly, this has stayed with me.)

Death is the ultimate engine of regret. There is no way I can ever make up for skipping her birthday, no way I can excuse saying "no" to a dying woman. You could say: regret is useless. You could say: what if, God forbid, your father-in-law had gotten killed crossing the street? Wouldn't you have regretted skipping HIS birthday? Even if he hadn't gotten killed, wouldn't your absence have been noted by your entire family, whereas Mildred was just a friend?

I can only answer by the fact that, all these years later, I still feel bad about the way that weekend shook out.

Maybe, in an alternate universe, we could each have three minutes to explain ourselves to the dead. Maybe the fact that, in our universe, we don't, encourages us to, in the words of that unfortunately all too accurate cliché, live each day as if it were our last. Well, yeah, wouldn't that be great. I have a friend who recently knelt on her dog's grave and, seriously in tears, begged her forgiveness for not throwing the orange squeaky toy enough the night before the dog succumbed to her final illness. Now that is what I call love!

I know a hospice nurse who insists that, when a dying person is comatose, hearing is the last sense to go. So she encourages family and friends to tell the person whatever they want or need to say. She may very well be bluffing. That talk is for the living.

You always hear about death bed protestations of love—as if family members did not love each other because, over the years, they were not in the habit of saying those actual words. I have another three words, and they are: that is baloney. Still, if it makes you feel good to insist that you love someone who has shared much or all of a life with you, go knock yourself out. You definitely don't want to get into the regret business.

Forgiveness is another story, and pretty much always a good one. If there is any good that come out of this final deadline, this final goodbye, it is the way it kicks us in the ass, prompting us to get over whatever it was that seemed important enough to keep us apart. In Mildred's case, there was not a lot of pent-up forgiveness necessary, and maybe now I should look into forgiving myself.

At the time, this is how I thought about things: my first twenty years I had my grandmother, Millie. My second twenty years I had Mildred. So I felt sad but lucky. And maybe that birthday business has helped me to make decisions about these kinds of issues with more confidence in the years since then.

Do I still miss Mildred? Not day to day. And the funny thing is that I have only one photo of her, which I only look at when I run across it in the photo box. But every time I go to their house (Jim remarried soon after; the house has done a stylistic 180, and yes, I do like Jill) I see the place the way it was before, and I feel good being there, remembering how I used to spend time with Mildred.

Can I just tell you one more thing? When it was lunchtime, Mildred would put together a concoction of leftovers she called Mildred's Mush. It came vaguely from their time in Rome, and you may recognize its starting point as spaghetti carbonara. Here is how it goes: Heat some olive oil in the pan, then add some leftover rice or pasta, whatever starch you find in the fridge. Add chopped up veggies, if you have any. Crack an egg over it, and stir it gently, low heat. Top it with parmesan. I also add pepper. It's warm, it's comforting, it's at once creative, exotic, homey and cheap, and it gives you something when you think you have nothing at all. I eat it quite often and, when I do, I see Mildred tooling around in her chair, with the laugh that seemed so hearty and large coming from such a small frame. The mush tastes that much better because she gave it to me.

How We Become *the* People We've Lost:
Winter Boots

ONE WINTER NOT TOO LONG AGO, I BOUGHT A PAIR OF ankle-height boots. Their squat, indented heel and fake fur cuff gave them a retro look, but I bought them not so much for looks as for comfort. The back problem I had a couple of years ago caused me to become addicted to clogs, not painkillers. They seem to set up my posture correctly, and give my back a fighting chance. When I saw that the clog people made a boot, it was a no-brainer, even though I already owned a reasonable pair of high winter boots. Since I have bought these clog boots, though, the reasonable high ones have never left the closet.

One day, I was walking in the downtown of a small city I had never been in before. It was windy and raw, I had the high collar of my down coat zipped way up around my neck, and I was wearing a winter hat. Of course I was wearing my wonderful boots.

And here is what happened: a new, clear image of my

mother emerged—from the streetscape, from my body, from the winds of the past. It was a combination of suddenly remembering her in a new way, feeling like her, thinking that I probably looked like her, feeling her presence in me and around me. It had to do with the way that I walked in the boots, the way that my coat was pulled up against the wind, the way that I walked purposefully down city streets.

My mother was thrilled to be a city girl. She grew up moving between several small eastern cities and, as soon as she could, established herself in New York. I went in the other direction, literally and sartorially. I moved north and, as an adult, become comfortable with winter sports, with dressing in layers of "performance" clothes. But it is when I am in a city, balancing in the middle of a rolling subway car, finding a shortcut between downtown buildings, eating a warm pretzel on the street, that I most sense my mother, the person who taught me to love all those things.

She had the city girl's sense of always being "on." Even if she was just walking around the corner to the butcher, she looked good. Even in the housedress she changed into when she came into the apartment, she looked good. When I was walking in those boots with my excellent posture, my quick city stride, my sense of stylish mastery—well, that was my mother in some way transmogrified through me.

This felt exciting. I hadn't had any new thoughts about my mother in years. But these weren't exactly thoughts, but more a sense of physical closeness. I am like her; she is in some weird way close to me. And that gave me a feeling of fullness, as well as a bubbly kind of peace.

I have never looked particularly like my mother; in coloring and facial structure I more took after my father's side. But as I've gotten older, sometimes when I glance in the mirror to wash my face or check on my hair, I am startled by a gust of the known, the remembered—around the eyes, or, again, the posture. I am probably four inches shorter than she was, so I don't have the presence. But we have the same broad shoulders and long arms. I don't have her big expressive personality. But now that I have gray hair, and my face has lost its roundness, a flash of her appears.

This kind of growing-into does not need a genetic component. We used to know a family who looked like the League of Nations: parents of Scandinavian descent whose adopted Asian and African-American children grew up with their blond-haired biological kids. More than once I caught myself wanting to tell one of the parents, So-and-So looks exactly like you, only to realize that it was biologically impossible. But why not? Old married couples are said to grow into each other's looks. It is the gesture, the posture, the attitude that we are talking about here.

And, to answer another question that you may or may not have been wondering about: why I have been going on about my friends, about my grandmother? What about Mom and Dad? The truth seems to be that, in some weird way, although they are long dead, they are never really gone from me. They are so much a part of who I am that having them disappear seems impossible. For many women, this is so much more true of the bond with our mothers. Little girls don't separate themselves from their mothers, who are, let's face it, for the most part, our primary caregivers and first love objects. We know from day one that we are not like our dads. But our moms? Too close to the bone.

Still, in some ways, we all become our dead parents. One friend hears her father's voice whenever she's at the meat counter, directing her to the nicer cut of lamb, or a New York strip steak. Another feels her mother's breath over her shoulder whenever she throws out a perfectly good, reusable piece of aluminum foil. A friend of mine who is chronically late decided to start wearing her dead husband's wristwatch. She finds it easier to get places on time now; she no longer feels she is hurrying to get somewhere alone.

It has been twenty years since my own mother died. I don't think about her a lot, or maybe it would be more accurate to say that I don't think about her a lot in a conscious way. But she is always here, always around, always available. She is present in the way that I stand, in the squaring of my shoulders (when I am standing properly), in the way that I pull up my collar to warm my neck.

I walk down the streets of a strange city and my mother walks—not with me or through me, but in some visceral way as part of me. That is just how it is, as if the concept of twenty years was no more substantial than the scrap of paper blown across the street by the fierce winter wind.

HOW ARE WE GOING *to* DIE?:
WHO *by* FIRE

*W*HEN I BEGAN GOING TO HIGH HOLIDAY SERVICES as an adult, the thing that most struck me was a line I would recall, semi-accurately, as: ". . . who shall live and who shall die, who by fire and who by sword," which refers to what we might expect in the coming year. The idea is that, in the ten days that begin with Rosh Hashanah and end with Yom Kippur (the period is also known as the Days of Awe), you have a last chance to return to goodness, make yourself one with God, act with righteousness and justice. If you do that, you stand a better chance of, among other things, not dying in the coming year.

Yikes. Although the concept that death could come out of anywhere, at any time, is obvious to anyone who is even half-awake to the world, to have it spelled out like that, recited in unison with a room full of people, really gets your attention.

Here is how the prayer book actually reads:

How many shall leave this world and how many shall be born into it, who shall live and who shall die, who shall live out the limit of his days and who shall not, who shall perish by fire and who by water, who by sword and who by beast, who by hunger and who by thirst, who by earthquake and who by plague, who by strangling and who by stoning, who shall rest and who shall wander, who shall be at peace and who shall be tormented, who shall be poor and who shall be rich, who shall be humbled and who shall be exalted.

But penitence, prayer and good deeds can annul the severity of the decree. (The decree about who shall live, etc.)

And of course I am thinking, even as I am joining in the recitation, isn't this a gross oversimplification? What about the people who were good, and who died since the last time I recited this very long affirmation? What about the selfish ones, the no-goodniks, the glum drags on the system who live on and on? And isn't that catalogue of the possible varieties of the end game an illusion or delusion, a way to let us think we have some infinitesimal hint of control over our destinies?

Yeah, so we know that we won't live forever. And we also know that people who are more wonderful in any number of ways don't necessarily live longer than those who are second or third rate. You can make a tenuous argument involving a better mental state promoting better health, or something about how, if you feel more positive about your life, you will take better care of yourself which might buy you a couple more minutes or months on this earth. But really. Even as we are acutely aware of the facts about reducing cholesterol or wearing seatbelts, we also know only too well about the bolt from the blue.

So why do we include this part of the liturgy year after year? And couldn't it use, at the very least, a little updating? Wouldn't it make more sense to say, *Who by cancer and who by car crash, who by falling off the roof and who by complications of diabetes, who by choice and who by freak accident, who by the sheer fact of old age?* But mammograms, reduction of salt intake, and careful driving can give us a minisculy better leg up against that awful decree of our impending death, even though we are being told that our faith in mammograms might be overblown.

Maybe doing good deeds helps you to sleep better at night, which maybe boosts your immune system. Maybe I will give you that. And I know about the research that shows that people who affiliate with a religious community do better in old age; that it's the affiliation rather than the spirituality that correlates with increased life expectancy. So maybe reciting these things in unison with others, even if we don't totally believe them, might actually do some good. Might. Some.

When I realized that I was actually writing this book, I idly thought: I wonder if anyone important to me will die while I am writing it? I wonder if I will have enough material? Because authors, the people who invented vampires, are the worst bloodsuckers of all. Who else could conceive of a situation that is so self-serving, while giving the appearance of conjuring our common humanity? It puts me in a very strange position—the more bad things happen, the better off I am (from a strictly professional point of view, of course).

I came to this project out of despair. It's not like I have any power over the end dates of those around me. My only choice is how I respond, what I do with the bad joke of existence. We connect, we connect, we connect. And then we lose, we lose, we lose.

Those losses accumulate relentlessly, year after year, each one reminding us of another. The people who populate our world die off and other new ones arrive. We haven't had time to get to know the newborns yet, or the people who have just moved into the neighborhood, or the potential friends who have recently crossed our paths, so we can only be happy about the most basic fact of their coming to join us. We don't yet know who these new people will turn out to be, how we will feel about them, what they will do.

But the people who die—ah, those are the ones whom we know intimately. We have been with them over time. They have taught us how to be, formed who we are, shared all of the things that have made up our lives. They are the warp to our woof, the knit to our purl. They are not the backdrop of our lives; they *are* our lives. And they will go on dying no matter how much we return to goodness, get close with God—yea, even though we do good deeds nonstop from the morning of the first day of the year to the night of the last.

The Canadian Jewish songwriter Leonard Cohen wrote a song, "Who By Fire," that takes as its starting point the language of that High Holiday prayer. It has the obsessively repetitive quality I have noticed in songs and poems that respond to the cruel fact of death, maybe because, in the face of it, we can do little more than rock back and forth on our heels. Cohen writes:

And who by fire, who by water,
who in the sunshine, who in the night time,

The next two verses continue the list, and each verse ends with, "and who shall I say is calling?" which, for me, evokes a conversation with a God we may or may not believe in, who may or may not be capable of doing anything about those decrees.

An opposite, though still incantatory approach, is the song "Breaths" by Birago Diop and Ysaye Barnwell. It is associated with Sweet Honey in the Rock, an a-capella group of black women.

Those who have died have never never left.
The dead are not under the earth.
They are in the rustling trees.
They are in the groaning woods.
They are in the crying grass.
They are in the moaning rocks.

That would mean that people don't really leave us when they die, an impulse I can understand but a belief that unfortunately I just cannot summon. Still, it gives us a way to at least paper over that unavoidable fact of "gone-ness." And while we are hurting, the song gives us something to do with our voice, something to do with our breath.

That is how I am thinking about it now. Death, the continual erosion of the people in our world, goes on and on. When it happens, when it hurts, we can only repeat our mantras, whether in song, in prayer or in poetry, in community or alone. "They are in the groaning woods. They are in the crying grass. They are in the moaning rocks." "But penitence, prayer and good deeds can annul the severity of the decree."

The decree being that we will be here after they are gone. The decree being that we will watch them depart, and for years, maybe forever, we will feel the emptiness that they have left behind.

So what do we do with our feelings, with our days? Rituals are the first cousins of obsession. They help us get from one place to another, from one state to the next. At the funeral, we tell ourselves that the person is not really gone. "We will always remember you," we sob. "You will always be with us." We etch on the gravestone: "Always in our hearts."

Always is a very long time. But the form gives us something to say. And maybe saying it again and again helps us get to the place where we can admit that they are not actually there. Even as we know that they will always be in our hearts, we also know that they will no longer occupy center space. They will get pushed—not really aside, but just nudged over a little bit, through the years, to make room for the new ones who come in. They will still be there in our hearts, in our memories, in our core. Maybe they will just take up less space.

Because next year others will follow them out of our lives, out of life. Whether by fire or by sword or by diabetes or by dementia, we do not know. Yet.

A year after my friend Mitch died (you remember Mitch, don't you? It was his sudden death that set me on the path of this book), our local Jewish community spent the High Holidays together once again. Mitch's absence was a real presence, like the worst of the fog in our seaside community, obscuring the air, making it hard to see. Still, we had made it through a fall, a winter, a summer. Now it was fall again.

The night after Yom Kippur, a group of us sat together outdoors in the unseasonably warm evening to discuss a book with the unbeatable title of *This Is Real And You Are Completely Unprepared*. The Jewish calendar goes a little bit crazy at this time of year. The High Holidays are followed quickly by Sukkot, a harvest holiday that we celebrate by eating our meals in special outdoor shelters—the Hebrew word for which is always translated as "booths," which is not helpful at all and which makes me think about conventions. These are temporary structures with roofs made only of vegetal materials. There has to be more shade than sun, but not so many branches, vines and harvest fruits as to block any rain; a reminder of the way that God provided shelters for us after our escape from Egypt.

The book describes it this way: "We sit in a house that is only the idea of a house, a house that calls attention to the illusory nature of all houses." But then the author says that there is a joy in this "realization that nothing can protect us. Nothing can save us from death, so it's no use defending ourselves. We may as well give up, and there is a wonderful release in this giving up."

Maybe I am constitutionally unable to go for this kind of wonderful release. But I can feel the softness of the evening, the warmth that comes from sitting in a circle on folding chairs in the welcoming dark. It had stayed light enough, given the street light and the moon, that, even as day slid into night, we were able to read outdoors. We talked about the ideas in the book, and about what we had just been through.

The night wasn't entirely clear, but we could see enough. We could see the garden. We could see the street. We could see each other. We could see the sky.

*W*OULDN'T YOU KNOW IT: IN BETWEEN THE TIME this book was written and when it was published, another of my dear friends up and died. I had carefully plotted out what writers call the arc of the book, the through-line, and was pretty satisfied with the semi-upbeat ending I managed to pull out. In real life, though, everything is fine until it is not.

Evy was my pal at summer camp, the summers that we were thirteen and then fourteen. We chose to bunk together. She remembered that I took the top bunk; I don't remember the bunk part at all. What I do remember was her hair—the crisp blond was so light that it made you think of white. We teased her that there was a place at the back of her neck where her hair had come in green, maybe from the creepy things that were growing in the lake. She, of course, could never quite see that far back under part of her hair to check it out. She was socially advanced; she had a boyfriend (a cute one!) at a time when that was beyond me. She had a funny way of spreading her hands wide and saying "cha CHA!" for emphasis. None of this explains why we were friends.

I think it was the way that she half went along with the green hair sham. She was up for fun, which, at that age, might have been reason enough. We were at a stage when I don't think we kids were all that differentiated from one another. My friends from that time remember me as always giggling; something you would probably not recognize if you were to meet me today. So maybe we were just friends because we were friends.

After our second summer together at camp, her family moved from Massachusetts, where I might conceivably have visited her in the off season, to far-off California. We probably wrote a few times and then separately moved on to whatever changes happened at an age where each year has the possibility of being a totally new life.

When we were in our mid-twenties and I was making documentary films, I had a show at a Massachusetts university. There, at the check-in table at the women's center, was Evy—hair still platinum, smile still broad.

"Mimi!" she shrieked. Nobody had called me Mimi in years. She was running the women's center, was living in the nearby small town, was married, with a baby. I was living in Cambridge, newly married as well. We promised to stay in touch; we never did.

Fast forward twenty-five or so years. I was sitting next to a stranger at a dinner party, running out of conversation. When she mentioned the name of her small town, Fairhaven, a light bulb went off. I asked her if she knew Evy; the woman replied that she was Evy's best friend. This time I didn't let it go. I called Evy, we met; our friendship was on again.

My son was a year younger than Evy's daughter. We told them about each other, because they had things in common, and because they were old enough that they didn't mind their mothers passing along information/meddling in their lives. (It helped that we had never met each other's kid.) In due time, the two of them married. Every step of the way, Evy and I giggled and said, wouldn't it be something if . . . they went out on a date . . . they really liked each other . . . etc., etc., etc., up through the two beautiful babies who turned us both into grandmothers.

In which capacity we were the same, but different. Which I think was okay with both of us. Evy loved when the girls exhibited the wild creature part of childhood; I liked doing domestic chores with them, maybe because I had spent so much of my time with my own grandmother cooking, baking, sewing, knitting.

By now you have figured out that this is not going to end well. Evy got breast cancer; hated the whole idea of the thing, didn't like to talk about it, got through it with as little to-do as possible. Then, a few years later, more bad news—ovarian cancer. And oddly, or luckily, given that her female line was now my progeny as well, she did not have the bad cancer gene.

Again, she did not like to talk about it. No wallowing. No obsessing. And I certainly did not like to think about it. I wondered if I was just avoiding it, or if maybe I was following Evy's lead, or if maybe, as a shrink friend said, I was dipping my toe into it little by little, as much as I could take, and there was nothing wrong with that.

Until she died quite suddenly, earlier than expected. An internal blockage, an especially bad one, a byproduct of the cancer. She was fine on a summer Thursday, when she checked out a super-long book from the library; she was dead that Saturday afternoon.

And I was the one who, while Evy was quickly dying in the hospital in Boston, with her immediate family filling her room, was muddling through as best I could with the two little girls. Evy's daughter Jana, my daughter-in-law, had called me anxiously late Friday morning: could I get down to Fairhaven to meet the bus that afternoon when Liza and Ruthie came home from day camp? (Our kids and grandkids had been spending much of the summer close to Evy. They knew that time with her might be limited.)

As the girls got off the bus, sunburned and dragging their huge backpacks, I thought that the news it would be my job to convey to them that weekend would only be bad, not tragic. What we were expecting was another hospital stay followed by more recuperating and resting at home.

So I went into my reassuring grandma mode. "Grandma Evy isn't feeling well, she's in the hospital in Boston. Your mommy and daddy are with her," I explained. But as we ate dinner at Friendly's, the quintessential Massachusetts fast food restaurant, a treat for these girls, I was sneaking off for a quick phone update. And later, as I tucked them into bed, I was telling them (they were six and eight) that Grandma Evy was very sick, sicker than we had been saying. I was laying the groundwork for what might be a much quicker schedule.

Their parents, my son and daughter-in-law, had, until this time, been managing the Grandma-is-sick timeline with a great deal of thought, but perhaps not enough imagination. They had never mentioned the D word to the girls. Jana and Eli were now fortyish, but this was the first time that they were on the front line of death. They thought that they still had months, maybe a year, of a slow decline. They did not realize (did not want to realize?) that death has a way of making fools of us all. And who could blame them? Who would want to tell these two perfect children that the world as they had known it was about to end?

The next morning, Saturday, Peter and I took the girls to a local museum that luckily had a kids' art project you could spend the morning on for an exorbitant extra sum. Money? Money was not an object if, for awhile, we could avoid think-ing about, talking about, the awful thing that was crowding out all the space in our minds.

As the girls painted, I huddled outside with my phone. At the end of the morning I had to tell them: Grandma is not coming home. Grandma is going to die.

There are so many bad parts about having our loved ones leave us. But this is one of the worst ones: having to break the hearts of those you love; having to tell children that, all along, you have been telling them lies. The world, indeed, is fragile. The world, indeed, can crack right open.

We moved through the next few days in that state that is both heightened and blurred. On a warm sun-drenched afternoon, the family held a memorial service in the back yard, prime season for Evy's garden. The girls stood up front for part of it, each holding a photo that Evy had taken. It gave them a way to be part of the service without having to speak.

A few days earlier, when Jana had come home from the

hospital and had broken the news that Evy had died that afternoon, her next words to the girls were, "Grandma Evy loves you very much." Present tense. Present tense. In our little world, Grandma Evy will always be present. She will be going "cha CHA!" She will be hiding little trinkets in her pockets for the girls to find. She will be yelling "Naked baby!" with glee. She will be grinning at me and saying, "Who would have thought? Who would have thought?"

ACKNOWLEDGMENTS

To my writing mafia: Liz Berge, Sally Brady, Michal Brownell, Anne Emerson, Alice Holstein, Jeanne Guillemin, Cindy Linkas, Chris Lynch, Betsy Seifter, Laura Wainwright, Patricia Welbourn; a million thanks.

ABOUT THE AUTHOR

photo credit: Lajla LeBlanc

MIRIAM WEINSTEIN has been a documentary filmmaker, a journalist, and a writer about topics related to family life, to food, and to Judaism. Her book, *The Surprising Power of Family Meals: How Eating Together Makes Us Smarter, Stronger, Healthier, and Happier*, helped spark a national conversation. Her book, *Yiddish: A Nation of Words*, won the National Jewish Book Award. She lives in Gloucester, Massachusetts, with her husband.

Follow her blog about grandparenting at
www.miriamweinstein.com

SELECTED TITLES FROM SHE WRITES PRESS

She Writes Press is an independent publishing company
founded to serve women writers everywhere.
Visit us at www.shewritespress.com.

Four Funerals and a Wedding: Resilience in a Time of Grief by Jill Smolowe.
$16.95, 978-1-938314-72-8. When journalist Jill Smolowe lost four family
members in less than two years, she turned to modern bereavement
research for answers—and made some surprising discoveries.

From Sun to Sun: A Hospice Nurse's Reflection on the Art of Dying by Nina
Angela McKissock. $16.95, 978-1-63152-808-8. Weary from the fear
people have of talking about the process of dying and death, a highly
experienced registered nurse takes the reader into the world of
twenty-one of her beloved patients as they prepare to leave this earth.

*Falling Together: How to Find Balance, Joy, and Meaningful Change
When Your Life Seems to be Falling Apart* by Donna Cardillo. $16.95,
978-1-63152-077-8. A funny, big-hearted self-help memoir that tackles
divorce, caregiving, burnout, major illness, fears, and low self-esteem
—and explores the renewal that comes when we are able to meet
these challenges with courage.

*Tell Me Your Story: How Therapy Works to Awaken, Heal, and Set You
Free* by Tuya Pearl. $16.95, 978-1-63152-066-2. With the perspective of
both client and healer, this book moves you through the stages of
therapy, connecting body, mind, and spirit with inner wisdom to
reclaim and enjoy your most authentic life.

Three Minus One: Parents' Stories of Love & Loss edited by Sean Hanish
and Brooke Warner. $17.95, 978-1-938314-80-3. A collection of stories
and artwork by parents who have suffered child loss that offers
insight into this unique and devastating experience.

Breathe: A Memoir of Motherhood, Grief, and Family Conflict by Kelly
Kittel. $16.95, 978-1-938314-78-0. A mother's heartbreaking account of
losing two sons in the span of nine months—and learning, despite all
the obstacles in her way, to find joy in life again.